Artificial Intelligence for Safety-Critical Automotive Applications

Navigating Functional Safety and Cybersecurity Standards for Safe AI Integration

Andy Gudera

November 2024

This book presents my personal interpretation of Artificial Intelligence and Functional Safety, with a particular focus on ISO 26262 for Functional Safety, ISO 21448 (SOTIF) for Safety of the Intended Functionality, ISO 21434 for Cybersecurity, and other relevant standards and regulations.

Contents

1. Abstract

The automotive industry simply cannot ignore certain trends in electronics, including artificial intelligence (AI). The ideas for artificial intelligence are not new, there was simply a lack of high-performance and at the same time affordable hardware.

Following Moore's Law, with the predicted doubling of integrated circuits from in IC's in a maximum of 24 months, performance and complexity have also increased considerably. The application of AI is also within reach for cars.

In the chapter 'Clarification of terms', I use the term Artificial Intelligence to illustrate the discrepancy between common usage and the actual content of the term.

Another trend in the automotive world is the desire to automate driving. I don't want to go into the reasons for this here. However, it becomes interesting when automated driving meets artificial intelligence.

With automated driving, there is a clear increase in the industry's understanding that safety is an important factor in the end user's acceptance of the technology.

In this paper, I try to provide at least some clarification in the jungle of terms and contexts surrounding the application of AI in safety-critical automotive applications.

For better recognition of automotive relevant shares, these are marked.

Part I.

Technical basics

2. Clarification of terms and technical background

2.1. Purpose and Technical Basis of Electronic Systems

Electronic systems are primarily designed to perform essential functions that form the backbone of modern technological applications.

These functions include:

- controlling[1]
- regulating[2]
- communicating[3]
- displaying[4]
- user interaction[5]

Together, these functionalities address the growing need for intelligent, adaptive, and user-friendly electronic systems.

These systems are widely employed across various domains. In industrial automation, they streamline production processes and ensure precision in operations.

---

[1] e.g., maintaining the desired speed of a car using cruise control to enhance safety and comfort for drivers

[2] e.g., keeping room temperature consistent via a thermostat in a heating system, which ensures energy efficiency and user comfort

[3] e.g., transmitting data between devices using Bluetooth or Wi-Fi, enabling seamless connectivity in smart homes and industrial IoT systems

[4] e.g., showing a car's speed on a digital dashboard, providing essential feedback to the user in real-time

[5] e.g., allowing a user to control a washing machine via a touch panel, making interfaces more intuitive and accessible

In consumer electronics, they simplify daily tasks through smart devices. The automotive sector leverages these systems to enhance vehicle performance and safety, while the aerospace industry relies on them for precise navigation and critical system monitoring. Each application showcases the versatility and indispensability of electronic systems in today's world.

The overarching purpose of these systems is to enable efficient and precise operation while enhancing safety, usability, and functionality.

2.1.1. Basic control loop

At the heart of these electronic systems lies in a foundational concept: control loop principles. [41, 4.2.3]

Control loops, often employed in regulating processes, operate by continuously measuring output, comparing it to a desired setpoint, and adjusting inputs accordingly to minimize errors.

This feedback mechanism is integral to ensuring stability and reliability, whether it's maintaining a car's cruise control speed or stabilizing a drone in flight.

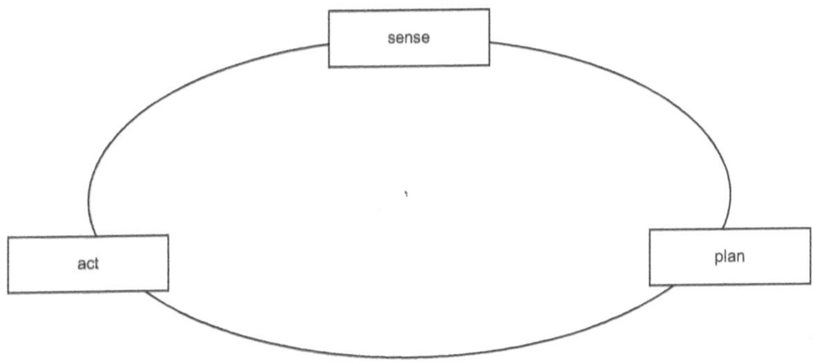

Fig. 2.1.: Control loop simple

The general structure of a control loop can be illustrated through the following block diagram, an illustration that can be found in any textbook on control technology.

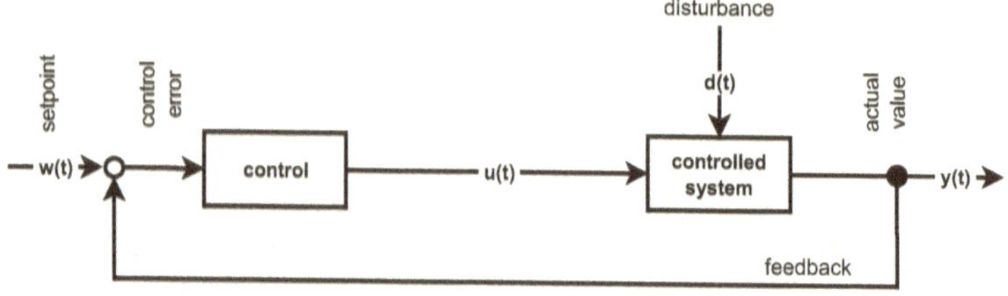

Fig. 2.2.: Control loop diagram

The controlled system in fig. 2.1 is the dynamic process following rules of physics that is subject to control actions aimed at maintaining a desired output.

It is not clear from this presentation how the regulation will be implemented. For example, the control could be implemented using a purely analogue circuit.

2.1.2. Digital control loop

So let's transfer the general illustration to the application of digital technology and it's specifics.

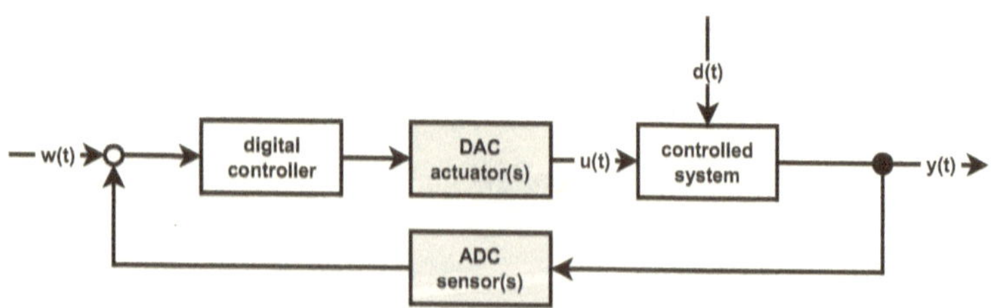

Fig. 2.3.: Control loop digital

In digital systems, continuous (analogue) signals are converted into discrete samples so that they can be processed in specific, sequential time steps. This transformation allows the system to handle and manipulate data using digital techniques, which are fundamental to modern control systems.

The digital controller operates through a combination of essential components, each of which plays a specific role in the overall functionality.

The framework illustrates a high-level interaction between the main elements:

SENSORS which collect data from the physical environment,

CONTROLLER which processes this information to determine appropriate actions and

ACTUATORS which execute these actions to influence the system under control.

Together, these components form a feedback loop that enables precise and responsive control of dynamic systems while ensuring robust operation under varying conditions.

2.1.3. Functional control loop

Control systems are not an end in themselves but are designed to fulfil specific purposes, ensuring that systems operate effectively and achieve their intended objectives.

From a functional perspective, control systems fulfill several primary tasks essential for the regulation of processes:

SIGNAL ANALYSIS This involves the acquisition and processing of input signals from sensors to assess the current state of the system. It includes filtering and interpreting the data to extract meaningful information.

CONTROL ALGORITHM Based on the analyzed signals, the control algorithm determines the necessary actions required to achieve the desired state. It translates inputs into commands that guide the system's behavior.

ACTUATOR HANDLING The actuator is responsible for implementing the control signals by adjusting the system's physical components, such as motors, valves, or other devices, to bring about the desired change.

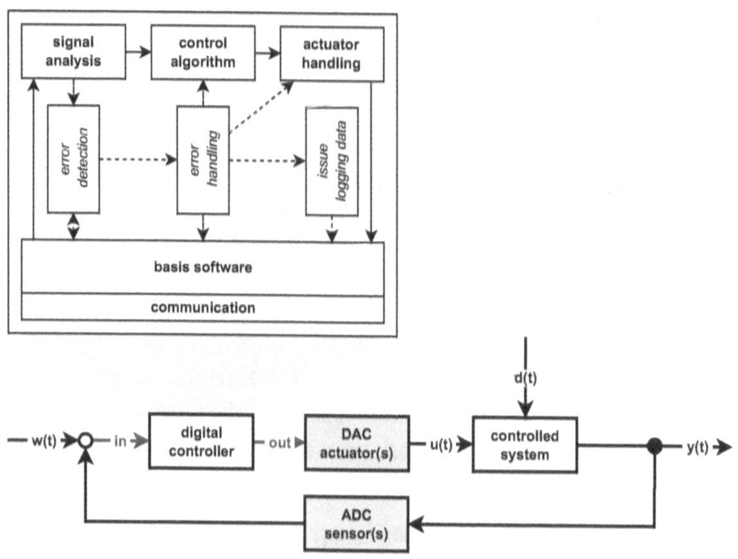

Fig. 2.4.: Control loop functional view

In addition to these primary tasks, control systems are often responsible for several secondary functions, which enhance their performance and ensure smooth operation:

ERROR DETECTION Monitoring the system for unexpected behavior or discrepancies, which could indicate faults or malfunctions, also known as self-diagnosis. Early detection is crucial to avoid system failures.

ERROR HANDLING When an error is detected, the system must take corrective actions, such as switching to a safe state or initiating recovery procedures.

ISSUE LOGGING Recording errors, system states, and operational anomalies for future analysis, troubleshooting, and improvement. This is usually referred to as fault memory.

INTERNAL AND EXTERNAL COMMUNICATION Ensuring that the control system can communicate effectively both within its internal subsystems[6] and with external devices or operators. This includes reporting errors, system status, and receiving external commands or feedback.

These tasks collectively ensure that the control system functions reliably and efficiently, adapting to both normal and exceptional conditions to maintain system stability and performance.

2.1.4. Software control loop

The next refinement of the control representation serves the purpose of seamlessly embedding the control logic in the controller software and in the OSI layer model.

This process involves taking high-level functional requirements, which typically describe what the system should do in broad terms, and breaking them down into a detailed software architecture that defines how these objectives will be met within the system.

This step involves specifying the individual software components, their responsibilities and the interactions between them.

---

[6]   e.g. to memory, bus driver, power semiconductors, intelligent sensors via SPI, I^2C, MLI

The translation process ensures that the software architecture meets both functional and non-functional requirements, such as performance, security and reliability. It may involve selecting appropriate design patterns, defining communication protocols, and deciding on data flow and control structures.

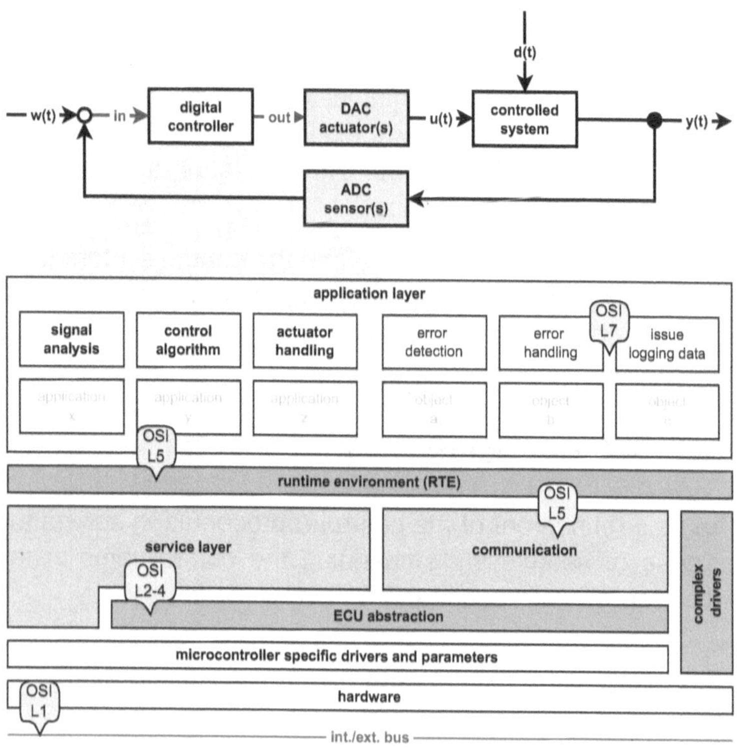

Fig. 2.5.: Control loop in generic software architecture

In addition, this phase often integrates considerations of scalability, maintainability and resource optimisation to ensure that the architecture is not only effective but also adaptable to future changes or extensions.

By bridging the gap between abstract requirements and actionable software design, this process establishes a clear, structured framework to guide subsequent implementation and verification efforts.

It ensures that every aspect of the software contributes to the overall objectives of the system, while respecting constraints such as hardware limitations or compliance with relevant standards.

2.1.5. Summary Electronic Systems

The reason for this exploration of control principles is to develop a deeper understanding of how artificial intelligence can be used effectively within control systems.

By examining the fundamental concepts and methods of classical control, such as feedback loops, signal analysis and actuator handling, it is possible to identify areas where AI technologies can enhance or transform these processes.

This understanding is particularly valuable in modern applications where the integration of AI with traditional control mechanisms can lead to more adaptive, intelligent and efficient systems capable of responding dynamically to complex and unpredictable environments.

2.2. Artifical Intelligence

The term Artificial Intelligence is initially the title of a grant proposal by the US-American computer scientist John McCarthy for a research project [51].

The content of the research project was a two-month study with 10 people, which should make it possible to describe aspects of learning and intelligence in such a way that it can be carried out by machines.

The term quickly entered common usage due to its catchiness and associated vision.

We are still a long way from the aim of being able to teach machines human-like intelligence. Here, the common usage of language proves to be a curse, as the expectations towards artificial intelligence do not correlate with the current technical possibilities.

So if you consider the term merely as a goal for technology and as a sub-field of computer science, or else as a media-effective advertising slogan, this is initially completely correct.

The field of sub-disciplines in AI is broad. For applications in the automotive sector, one can concentrate on the following disciplines:

- Pattern recognition including speech recognition and handwriting recognition
- Machine Learning (ML)
- Artificial neural networks and deep learning
- Computer vision

2.3. Machine Learning

There is no generally accepted definition of . Machine Learning (ML). However, both the German and English Wikipedia entries provide definitions that capture the essence of the term in a way that seems appropriate for this discussion.

ML refers to the process of generating knowledge through experience, with machines drawing on past data and experience to improve their performance over time [48]. Specifically, it involves the creation of algorithms that allow systems to learn autonomously, enabling them to refine their processes and adapt to new data or environments with minimal human intervention [48].

The field of machine learning encompasses a variety of approaches and methods, each suitable for different types of problems and data. In this text, only the most relevant aspects of these methods are briefly discussed to provide a context for further exploration [8].

2.3.1. Supervised machine learning

The method of supervised machine learning involves training an algorithm to identify and assign hidden patterns in data to specific, predefined output values.

This process relies on *labelled* data, where each data point is already associated with a known output, or 'label,' which acts as a guide for the learning process.

During training, the algorithm analyzes these examples, recognizing patterns or features that consistently correlate with certain outputs. This allows the model to 'learn' how to map new, unseen inputs to the correct outputs based on the patterns it has detected in the training data [85][73].

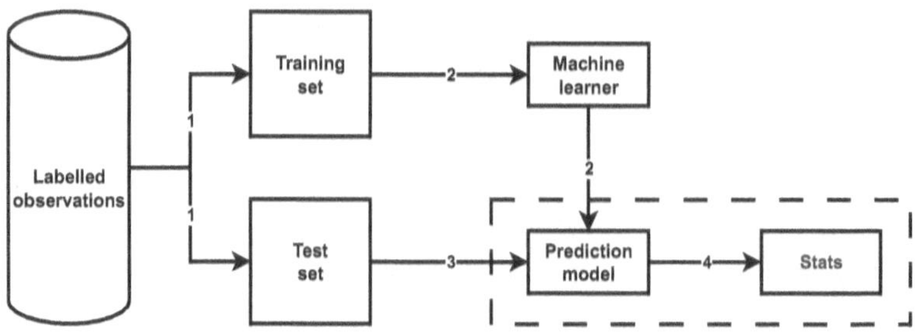

Fig. 2.6.: Supervised ML [63]

Supervised learning is widely used for tasks where clear input-output relationships are essential, such as image classification, where the algorithm learns to associate images with specific labels (e.g., 'cat' or 'dog'), or for predicting numerical values, like housing prices based on features such as location and size.

The primary goal is to minimize the difference between the model's predictions and the actual labels, which is achieved by optimizing the algorithm through repeated exposure to the labelled data.

One key aspect of supervised learning is the continuous feedback provided to the model during training. This feedback allows the algorithm to adjust its internal parameters iteratively, refining its accuracy with each iteration until it can reliably make predictions on new data that closely match the predefined labels.

Advantages

- easy to understand
- data only necessary for training the model
- known number of classes
- verifiable results[7] of the learning process

---

[7]   validation process

- specific output with measurable accuracy
- improvement of accuracy in prediction by additional
  training possible

Disadvantages

- large amounts of training data required
- learning without any prior knowledge
- less accuracy
- time-consuming, because data will be analysed in all
  directions
- clustering cannot be predicted or controlled

Typical algorithms

- Naïve Bayes
- linear regression
- logistic regression
- support vector machines (SVM)
- K-nearest neighbor (KNN)
- random forest

Conceivable or typical applications

- stock market predictions
- biometric patterns
- speech recognition, e.g. Siri
- search engines, e.g. Google search
- spam detection
- object detection

2.3.2. Unsupervisesd machine learning

The ML algorithms in unsupervised learning are designed to
analyze and cluster *unlabelled* datasets by detecting hidden
patterns and structures without the need for human intervention or pre-existing labels. This approach allows the algorithm

to explore the data freely, identifying natural groupings, correlations, or patterns that may not be immediately obvious.

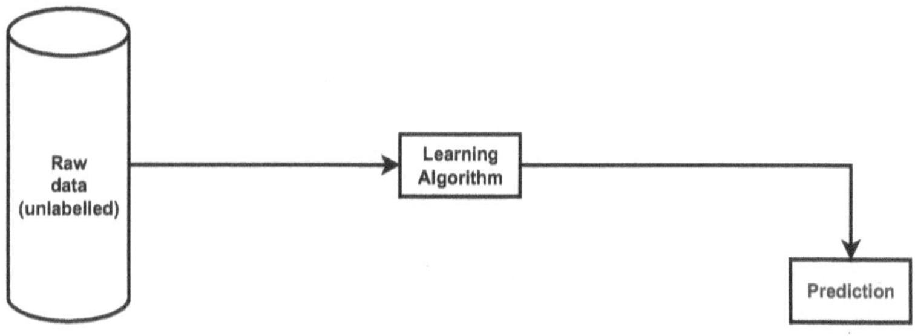

Fig. 2.7.: Unsupervised ML [78]

One common technique in this area is clustering[8], where groups of unlabelled data points are examined for underlying similarities or differences.

The algorithm organizes these data points into clusters, with each cluster representing a set of items that are more similar to each other than to those in other clusters [87][74].

In addition to clustering, unsupervised learning includes other techniques such as association (identifying relationships among variables) and dimensionality reduction (reducing the number of variables while retaining key information).

These methods are particularly useful in fields like customer segmentation, anomaly detection, and recommendation systems.

In this way, unsupervised machine learning mirrors certain aspects of human learning behavior . Just as humans can often recognize patterns or group objects based on their attributes without explicit guidance, unsupervised learning algorithms can independently discover and organize patterns within large datasets.

---

[8]   a data mining technique commonly used in unsupervised learning

This process not only aids in data analysis but also uncovers new insights that may inform future supervised learning models or guide decision-making.

Advantages

- no effort in labelling data sets
- finding of hidden patterns
- can help to understand raw data[9]

Disadvantages

- huge amount on data necessary
- learning without any prior knowledge
- less accuracy
- time-consuming, because data will be analysed in all directions
- clustering cannot be predicted or controlled

Typical algorithms

- K-nearest neighbor
- clustering
  - K-means
  - hierarchical clustering
  - principal components analysis, singular value decomposition
- unsupervised neural network
  - generative adversarial networks (GAN)
  - autoencoder (AE)

Conceivable or typical applications

- genome analyses
- data preprocessing
- credit cards fraud detection

---

9   e.g. degree of similarities of data using probabilistic methods

2.3.3. Reinforcement machine learning

Reinforcement Learning (RL), is a method for solving sequential decision problems that are often associated with a high degree of uncertainty [56].

In this paradigm, an autonomous software agent learns to make a series of decisions by exploring its environment, discovering which actions lead to desired outcomes, and optimising its behaviour to achieve or maximise rewards over time.

To do this, the agent must develop a strategy or 'policy' that guides its actions in different situations. A policy in RL is essentially a mapping from states (or situations) in the environment to actions that the agent should take.

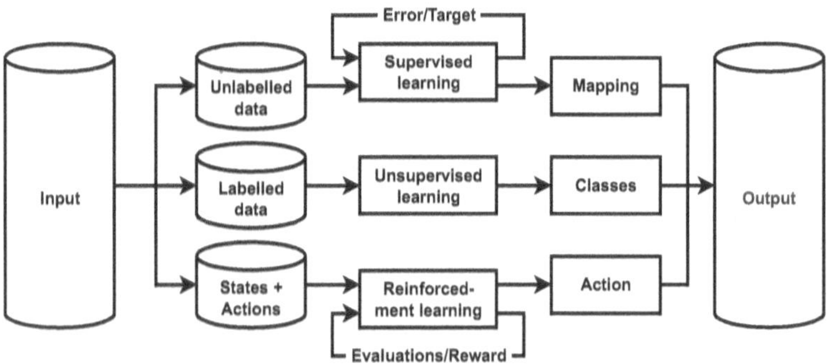

Fig. 2.8.: Reinforcedment ML [75]

This policy is learned incrementally through trial and error, without direct human guidance, based solely on feedback from the environment.

Positive feedback (rewards) reinforces actions that lead to favourable outcomes and encourages the agent to repeat them, while negative feedback (punishments or penalties) discourages undesirable actions [13].

That process, known as exploration and exploitation, is central to reinforcement learning. The agent must explore different actions to understand their consequences (exploration), but also apply its learned policy to maximise rewards based on previous experience (exploitation).

This balance is crucial, as focusing solely on exploration can lead to inefficient learning, while overemphasis on exploitation can cause the agent to miss potentially better actions.

Reinforcement learning has become a powerful tool in domains where real-time decision making is essential, such as robotics, autonomous vehicles, and even complex strategy games. In these domains, the agent is often faced with dynamic and complex environments where immediate actions can have long-term consequences.

By interacting with its environment and continuously refining its policies, the agent gradually improves its ability to make optimal decisions.

In addition, reinforcement learning mimics certain aspects of human and animal learning behaviour, where positive and negative consequences shape future actions.

This learning-by-doing approach enables RL agents to develop sophisticated strategies that can adapt to new or changing environments, making reinforcement learning an invaluable method for tackling complex, uncertain problems.

Advantages

- no specific training data necessary
- finding their own solutions without human input
- solving complex control and optimisation problems with comparatively simple principles [54]

Disadvantages

- very computationally intensive
- slow simulation environments
- very complex definition of reward-engineering [13]
- high potential for disruptions[10] [13]

Conceivable or typical applications

- offboard navigation

2.3.4. Ensemble machine learning

Ensemble machine learning harnesses the power of combining multiple individual models to improve overall predictive performance. This technique is particularly useful when individual models tend to overfit or underperform on certain subsets of data.

By aggregating predictions from multiple models, ensemble methods help to minimise bias, reduce variance and improve model accuracy, especially in cases where data is noisy or complex. The two main approaches to *ensemble learning* are bagging (short for bootstrap aggregating) and boosting.

Bagging generates multiple models by training each one on a different subset of the training data generated by bootstrapping (sampling with replacement). The predictions of these models are then averaged (for regression tasks) or tuned (for classification tasks).

The best known bagging method is the Random Forest algorithm, which builds multiple decision trees and averages their predictions to reduce overfitting while maintaining accuracy.

---

[10] Reinforcement learning can lead to potentially ethically or economically questionable solutions. Depending on the reward engineering, the agent may be able to optimise without ethical or economic guidance.

In contrast, *boosting* trains models sequentially, with each new model correcting the errors made by the previous one. It focuses more on the misclassified data points in the training set, gradually improving accuracy.

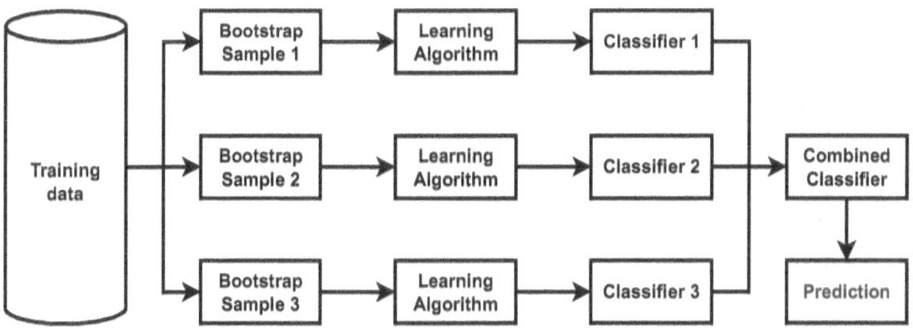

Fig. 2.9.: Bagging Flow [83]

Common boosting algorithms include AdaBoost [16], Gradient Boosting [49, 80] and XGBoost [80]. Boosting tends to be more sensitive to noise, but when tuned properly, it can outperform other methods in terms of predictive power.

Both approaches have their pros and cons. Bagging generally works well for high variance models (e.g. decision trees), while boosting is often better at improving the performance of weak learners.

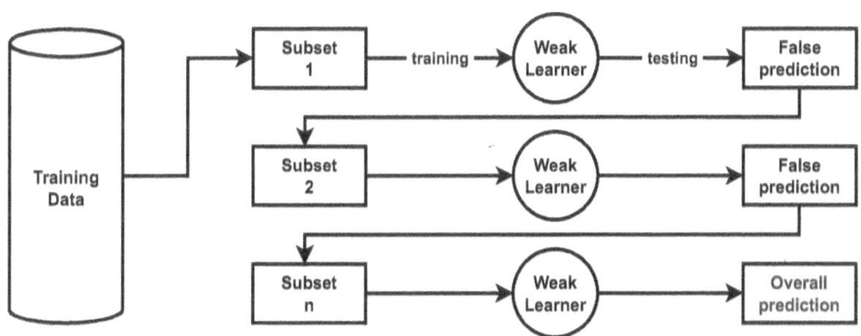

Fig. 2.10.: Boosting [71]

Together, they demonstrate the power of ensemble learning in creating robust models that are more reliable in making predictions across diverse datasets.

For a more in-depth exploration of ensemble methods, see resources such as [90] and [83].

Advantages

- increased predictive accuracy
- increased robustness to noise and outliners
- reduction of overfitting

Disadvantages

- increased complexity
- increased computing performance
- increased memory usage
- decreased interpretability

Conceivable or typical applications

- text classification
- image/voice recognition
- health care
- fraud detection
- anomaly recognition, cyber security

2.4. Deep Learning

Deep learning [64] is actually a subset or extension of ML, but it differs in that it mimics the neural processes of the human brain in a much more sophisticated way. While traditional ML focuses on identifying patterns in data and making predictions based on those patterns, deep learning aims to replicate the complex structure and functionality of the human brain's neural networks.

This enables deep learning models to perform more intricate and nuanced tasks, such as image recognition, natural language processing and complex decision-making.

One of the key differences between deep learning and traditional Machine Learning is the size and complexity of the models involved. Deep learning models, which are typically built using multi-layer neural networks, require far more computing power to train and optimise.

These models often consist of millions of parameters that need to be tuned during the training process. As a result, deep learning requires much more advanced hardware, such as Graphics Processing Units (GPUs) or specialised accelerators, to handle the immense number of calculations involved.

In addition to computing power, deep learning also requires much larger data sets to achieve high levels of accuracy. While traditional ML algorithms can be effective with smaller amounts of labelled data, deep learning models thrive on *large datasets* because they are able to automatically learn more complex features and representations from the data without the need for manual feature engineering.

This is why deep learning has been so successful in fields such as computer vision and natural language processing, where huge amounts of data are available to train models.

Deep learning's ability to handle large amounts of data and complex features makes it particularly powerful for applications that require human-level performance, such as autonomous driving, speech recognition and medical diagnostics.

However, it also presents significant challenges, including the need for large computational resources, data storage, and the potential for overfitting if the model is not properly regularised.

In summary, deep learning is an advanced and powerful extension of ML, but it requires significantly more computational resources and training data to reach its full potential.

Its ability to model complex patterns and features in large datasets allows it to tackle tasks that were previously difficult or impossible for traditional ML algorithms.

Advantages

- automatic feature extraction[11]
- better scalability
- higher prediction accuracy
- adaptive learning[12]

Disadvantages

- high computing performance and memory required
- high amount on training data
- high energy consumption

Conceivable or typical applications

- image recognition
- speech recognition
- natural voice processing
- medical imaging
- recommendation systems
- advertising
- content generation

---

[11]   learning of complex features from raw data without engineering steps
[12]   usage of adaptive learning strategies leads to continuos prediction performance improvement

2.5. Neural Network architectures

Depending on the application, different AI architectures are used to maximise effectiveness and efficiency. Each architecture offers unique benefits to meet the needs of tasks such as image recognition, natural language processing or real-time decision making.

This tailored approach allows developers to select the most appropriate models to achieve optimal performance and meet the specific requirements of different applications.

2.5.1. Artificial neural network

Neural network are an important subset of Machine Learning and form the basis for advances in deep learning.

Inspired by the structure and processes of the human brain, neural networks mimic biological neural networks to perform complex computational tasks. The core elements of neural networks, known as nodes, represent artificial neurons that resemble the natural neurons of the brain.

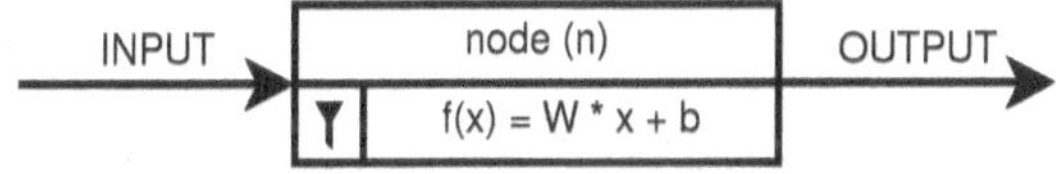

▼...activation function, x...INPUT, W...Weights, b...Bias vectors

Fig. 2.11.: Single node

These nodes are organised into layers, starting with an input layer, followed by one or more hidden layers, and ending with an output layer. Each layer is interconnected, allowing the network to process and learn from data through weighted connections that adjust during training to improve accuracy and performance.

This architecture enables neural networks to identify patterns, make decisions and perform predictive analysis, making it invaluable for a wide range of applications across industries.

The nodes in a neural network are interconnected, allowing information to pass from one node to the next through weighted links [82]. Organised into layers - input, hidden and output - these nodes each act as small computational units with two main components: the weighted sum and the activation function.

The weighted sum combines inputs from previous nodes, emphasising or de-emphasising features based on learned weights, while the activation function introduces non-linearity, enabling complex pattern recognition.

The number of nodes depends on the application; too few can lead to underfitting, missing important patterns, while too many can lead to overfitting, where the model learns too specifically from training data and struggles with new data.

The programming and implementation of these nodes is typically managed using powerful libraries such as TensorFlow, PyTorch and Keras, which provide pre-built tools and modules to streamline the creation of neural network models.

These libraries offer extensive functionality, including efficient tensor operations, model training utilities, and ready-to-use layers and activation functions, all of which simplify the complex process of defining and tuning networks.

In addition, AutoML frameworks and toolkits - such as NVIDIA DRIVE Constellation for autonomous vehicle simulation, H2O.ai Driverless AI, IBM Watson AutoAI and DataRobot - provide higher level automation. These tools can handle aspects such as hyperparameter tuning, feature selection, and model optimisation, helping both novice and expert users build robust AI models faster and more efficiently.

They support scalability and often come with built-in solutions to common AI development challenges, making them invaluable for those working on complex projects.

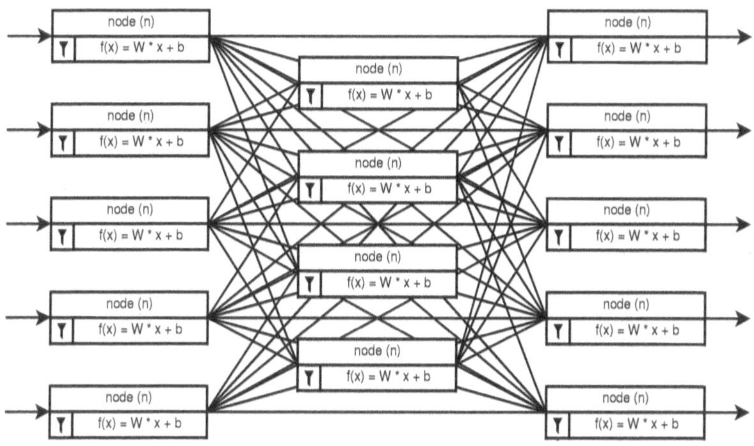

Fig. 2.12.: Node cluster

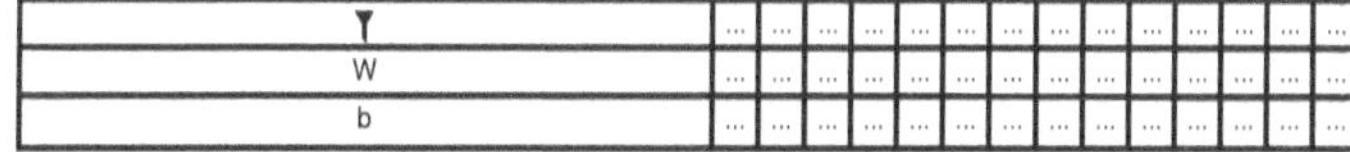

Fig. 2.13.: Node cluster parameter set

The exact function plugged in to each separate node depends on the aim of the application. However, typical functions are:

- activation function[13] (weighting function)
- backpropagation (updating/adjusting weights)
- optimisation algorithm[14] (error minimization)
- convolutional neural network

---

[13] e.g. sigmoid function, the tanh function, the rectified linear unit (ReLU) function, and the softmax function

[14] e.g. stochastic gradient descent (SGD), Adam optimizer, RMSprop optimizer, and Adagrad optimizer

Stimuli for the nodes are the exceeding of stimulus thresholds (threshold value). These lead to the transfer of data to the linked nodes. Without a stimulus, no data transfer takes place.

Neural networks can be implemented in hardware (PNN) or virtually (SNN). The implementation, however, is anything but trivial, despite the speaking name. This makes it all the more difficult to understand the technical realisation.

Conceivable or typical applications

- image recognition
- speech recognition
- natural disaster prediction
- financial analysis
- medical diagnostics
- text analysis, text processing

2.5.2. Convolutional neural network

A convolutional neural network (CNN) is a special type of neural network designed specifically for processing and extracting meaningful features from image data. Unlike traditional neural networks, which treat input data in a fully connected fashion, CNNs use a series of *convolutional layers* to scan small regions of an image at a time.

This structure allows CNNs to capture spatial hierarchies in the data by learning patterns at multiple levels, from simple edges to complex shapes and objects.

The core building block of a CNN is the *convolutional layer*, which uses a set of trainable filters (or kernels) to detect specific patterns in the input image. As these filters move across the image, they generate *feature maps* that highlight important features in each region. In early layers, CNNs typically learn to recognise basic visual elements such as edges, lines and textures.

As the network depth increases, it can recognise more abstract features and even detect complex structures, making CNNs highly effective for tasks such as image classification, object detection and face recognition. [47]

Conceivable or typical applications

- image recognition
- video analysis

2.5.3. Recurrent neural network

A recurrent neural network (RNN) is a type of neural network architecture specifically designed to process and analyse sequential data, including time series data, speech and other data ordered by sequential relationships.

Unlike traditional feedforward neural networks, RNNs have an internal memory structure that allows them to retain information from previous steps or elements in a sequence.

This is essential for tasks where the context of earlier data points influences the interpretation of later data points, such as speech recognition, language modelling and time series forecasting.

To achieve this, RNNs are constructed with loops, or feedback connections, that allow information to be passed from one step in the sequence to the next. These feedback links form a directed cycle in the network, effectively creating a memory of previous computations.

At each time step, the hidden state of the network is updated, taking into account both the current input and the hidden state from the previous time step. This recursive updating allows

RNNs to maintain a form of temporal context, making them uniquely suited to sequential data processing. [24]

Conceivable or typical applications

- natural disaster prediction
- financial analysis
- text analysis, text processing
- machine translations

2.5.4. Generative adversarial networks

Another type of neural network used for unsupervised learning is the GAN. In this architecture, two competing networks, a *generator* and a *discriminator*, are trained in an adversarial setup.

The *generator* aims to create new, seemingly realistic data samples, such as images, by learning from the distribution of a given data set. Its goal is to generate data that is as close to the real data as possible, effectively trying to 'fool' the discriminator.

The *discriminator*, on the other hand, is designed to evaluate the authenticity of the data by distinguishing between real data (from the dataset) and fake data (produced by the generator). Through this adversarial process, both networks continuously improve: the generator becomes better at generating realistic data, and the discriminator becomes better at identifying generated data.

This competition between the generator and the discriminator drives the generator to produce increasingly realistic data over time, as it constantly tries to outsmart the discriminator. This approach has led to impressive advances in image synthesis, video generation, and other creative applications. [4][6]

Conceivable or typical applications

- image generation and image high resolution upscaling
- face generation
- video synthesis
- voice synthesis
- medical imaging
- AI generated art

2.5.5. Transformer

The transformer neural network is characterised by mechanisms based on *attention*. Attention mechanisms allow the model to focus on different parts of the input sequence with different degrees of importance, allowing it to capture long-range dependencies more effectively than traditional recurrent models.

The core idea behind attention is that any element in the sequence can interact with any other element, and these interactions are weighted according to their relevance to the current processing step.

The transformer model typically consists of several layers, each containing two primary components: *self-attention* and *feed-forward networks*. In the *self-attention* mechanism, each token in the input sequence attends to every other token, and the resulting weighted representations are used to update the token's own representation.

This allows the transformer to capture complex relationships between tokens regardless of their position in the sequence. The *feed-forward networks* within each layer perform further transformations on the output of the attention mechanism, introducing non-linearity and improving the expressiveness of the model.

One of the major advantages of the transformer model is its ability to *scale well*. Because the attention mechanisms are computed independently for each token in parallel, the model is well suited to modern hardware accelerators such as GPUs and TPUs, allowing efficient training on large datasets.

This parallelism makes the transformer model much faster to train than sequential models such as RNNs or LSTMs. In addition, transformers can handle sequences of arbitrary length, making them highly flexible for tasks such as machine translation, text summarisation and language modelling.

As a result, transformers have become the foundation of many state-of-the-art models, such as Bidirectional Encoder Representations from Transformers (BERT), Generative Pretrained Transformer (GPT) and T5, achieving significant improvements in a variety of natural language processing tasks. [79]

Conceivable or typical applications

- Bidirectional Encoder Representations from Transformers (BERT)
- Generative Pretrained Transformer (GPT)

2.6. Algorithms

The algorithms used by AI serve as the instructions for action that a *node* in a NN processes to determine whether the input data at the appropriate layer[15] exceeds the required thresholds to produce the resulting data that is passed on to other nodes in the network.

Each *node* in a neural network typically performs a mathematical operation, such as applying an activation function to the weighted sum of its inputs. The activation function helps

---

[15] input layer, hidden layer, or output layer

decide whether the node should 'fire' and send its output to the next layer.

The decision as to whether the input data exceeds a threshold is based on these calculated values, which determine the strength and direction of the signal passed to subsequent layers.

These algorithms can be assigned to the respective *nodes* and pre-parameterised through the use of *frameworks*. A *framework* is a set of tools and libraries that provide the necessary infrastructure for designing, training and deploying machine learning models, including neural networks.

Frameworks such as TensorFlow, PyTorch and Keras provide predefined algorithms, functions and methods for configuring and optimising nodes within a neural network. They simplify the process of setting up and training neural networks, allowing researchers and practitioners to focus more on model design and experimentation.

However, the actual (final) parameterisation of the nodes is typically done iteratively through the process of *ML* training. During training, the neural network adjusts its parameters (such as weights and biases) to minimise the error between the predicted outputs and the actual target outputs.

This process is typically performed using optimisation algorithms, such as gradient descent, which update the parameters based on the calculated error or loss.

Over multiple iterations, the network fine-tunes its parameters to improve accuracy and generalisation, ultimately producing a model capable of making accurate predictions on unseen data.

2.7. Big Data

First of all, in the vernacular, big data has become a buzzword that is difficult for outsiders to grasp, but whose lack of understanding is not something they want to admit.

Big Data refers to a constantly growing amount of data sets that are extremely large, fast-moving or complex. With traditional techniques, this data is difficult or impossible to analyse because the relationships behind the data are often unknown.

Doug Laney has defined Big Data in his 3-V model [46], which roughly means as much as: [84]

VOLUME - Vast amounts of data are constantly being generated from a variety of sources, including transactions, IoT devices, video and social media.

These data sets can be massive, often reaching petabytes or exabytes, making them difficult to store and process without the use of advanced technologies.

The rapid decline in storage costs over time has facilitated the processing and collection of such vast amounts of data[16] from multiple environments[17].

VELOCITY - The speed at which data is generated, processed and analysed is constantly increasing, driven by the rise of real-time analytics and automated decision-making systems.

Data streams are often ephemeral, requiring quick responses and immediate insights. This constant influx of fast data requires agile and scalable infrastructures to keep pace with the growing demands of businesses and applications.

---

[16]   made possible by low storage costs
[17]   e.g. transactions, intelligent devices (IoT), video, social media

VARIETY - Data now arrives in an increasing number of formats, ranging from structured data in databases to unstructured data such as text, images and video.

These different forms of data require specialised techniques for integration, processing and analysis. The variety of data sources and formats poses significant challenges in ensuring interoperability and extracting valuable insights across disparate systems.

In the context of artificial intelligence, big data represents a wealth of analysis possibilities, but also training data.

3. Development of AI components

After clarifying what AI is, it is now time to look at the actual application. What process or workflow must take place in order to be able to use artificial intelligence?

Since we are looking at automotive applications, I will try to limit myself to the relevant parts.

3.1. Development/selection algorithms

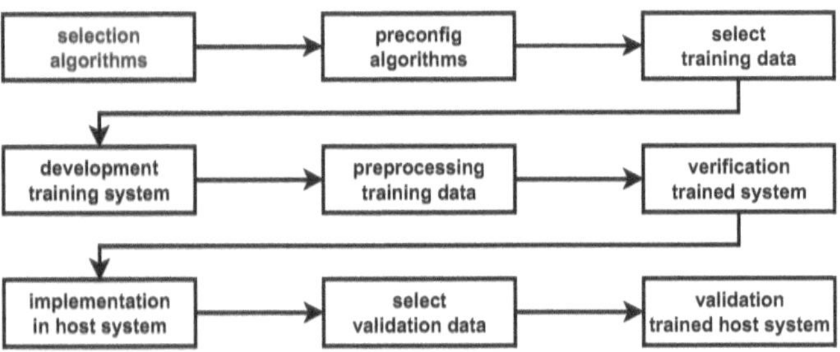

Fig. 3.1.: Selection Algorithm

As can be seen from the previous considerations, the *algorithms* or algorithmic concepts to be used in a given context depend on a variety of parameters.

These parameters can include, but are not limited to, the computational resources available, the required speed and accuracy, the type and amount of data to be processed, as well as the specific constraints and goals of the system.

The selection of an appropriate algorithm is not a one-size-fits-all decision but must be tailored to meet the specific needs and conditions of each application.

To better understand how these parameters influence the choice of algorithms, two examples from the automotive industry will be considered. These examples serve as practical cases where different algorithmic concepts must be applied depending on the operational environment and requirements.

OFFBOARD NAVIGATION In this example, navigation algorithms are executed *offboard*, meaning they run on powerful servers at an Original Equipment Manufacturer (OEM) or service provider via online connectivity.

These servers typically have access to extensive computational resources, enabling the use of more complex algorithms that might require significant processing power and large amounts of data. The system is capable of using high-precision maps, real-time traffic data, and other external sources of information to calculate optimal routes.

The key parameters here include the availability of cloud-based resources, high-speed data transmission, and the need for frequent updates.

Algorithms for this application may rely on machine learning models or graph-based search algorithms, which need to process large amounts of real-time data to make accurate predictions and route calculations.

TRAFFIC SIGN RECOGNITION In contrast, traffic sign recognition in a vehicle is executed *locally*, directly on a control unit within the vehicle. There's no online connectivity required.

So it requires a completely different approach in terms of computational resources and algorithm design.

Since the vehicle's control unit typically has limited processing power compared to cloud servers, the algorithms need to be efficient in terms of both computation and memory usage. Additionally, the system must operate in real time and process image data from cameras or sensors to recognize traffic signs as the vehicle moves.

The key parameters for this application include real-time performance, accuracy, and the ability to handle noisy sensor data.

Algorithms used here are likely to include deep learning models, such as convolutional neural networks (CNNs), which can efficiently classify and recognize traffic signs from images captured by the vehicle's cameras.

Both of these examples highlight how the choice of algorithm and the underlying computational architecture are influenced by the parameters of the system.

Offboard navigation systems can leverage the power of cloud computing to run more complex algorithms, while traffic sign recognition systems must be optimized for real-time processing on embedded systems with limited resources.

These contrasting scenarios demonstrate how different parameters, such as computational resources, data sources, and system constraints, directly impact the algorithm selection and design process in automotive applications.

When we think about autonomous driving, it is also possible to think about trajectory calculation, i.e. path planning within the range of the sensors based on AI.

The algorithms resulting from the requirements must either be programmed in case of unavailability or selected in corresponding frameworks.

Requirements	Offboard Navigation	Object Recognition
• type of data provided	• current location, destination • map data • traffic density	• video stream
• learning method	• unsupervised learning[1]	• supervised learning[2]
• prediction accuracy	• medium[3]	• high[4]
• scalability, efficiency	• high scalability[5]	• high efficiency[6]
• availability of libraries	• libraries for server applications needed	• libraries for embedded applications needed
• required resources, infrastructure	• GPS for position • HMI for destination and route visualization • internet connection • V2X information[7] • backend server with map and traffic information	• ECU with camera • vehicle network to HMI

---

[1] makes it possible to find unforeseen solutions

[2] limits the search for solutions to predefined patterns

[3] slight deviations from the ideal route are hardly ascertainable for the customer; a little better than competitors

[4] speeding could result in fines and dissatisfied customers

[5] at the same time, many customers must be able to navigate

[6] application in the vehicle must not consume a lot of resources

[7] traffic lights, car parks, electronic beacons, car2car traffic information, etc.

3.2. Preconfiguration algorithms

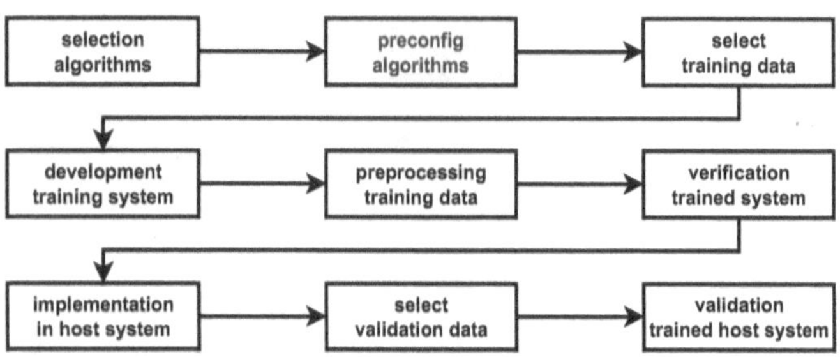

Fig. 3.2.: Preconfiguration Algorithm

AI algorithm often needs to be *pre-configured* for several reasons:

Efficiency and time saving

Many AI algorithms, especially in machine learning, require a set of hyperparameters (e.g. learning rate, number of layers, etc.) to be defined before training. This pre-configuration helps to **speed up the training process** and **optimise performance**.

Optimisation

Some algorithms require parameter tuning to achieve optimal results. Without pre-configuration, the learning process could be either very slow or completely ineffective.

Specific requirements of the use case

Different AI applications (e.g. image classification, speech processing, recommendation systems) require different algorithms and parameters tailored to the task.

Pre-selection of these ensures that the algorithm is appropriate for the specific use case.

Experience and Best Practices

Pre-configuration is based on best practice and previous experience, which indicates which parameters and models work best for specific datasets and tasks. This reduces the need to configure everything from scratch and leads to faster results.

Hyperparameters

Hyperparameters are:

NUMBER OF HIDDEN LAYERS AND NEURONS as a measure of complexity and capacity.

LEARNING RATE as the step size with which the model adjusts its weights during training.

BATCH SIZE which indicates how many training examples are required to change the weights.

REGULARISATION FACTOR as the adjustment of the balance between model complexity and information loss[8].

ACTIVATION FUNCTION as the enabler for nodes or neurons.

The hyperparameters thus determine the start of the learning or training process and are therefore essential for prediction. In practice, the determination of these parameters can be achieved by varying and parallel training.

---

[8] When there is a strong regularisation, less information is output by the AI

In summary, pre-configuration ensures efficient and targeted training of the AI, optimising the algorithm for the specific use case and reducing development effort.

3.3. Selection training data

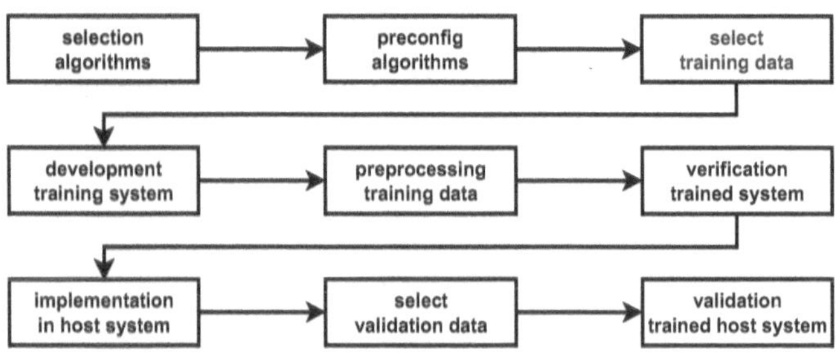

Fig. 3.3.: Selection Training Data

The training data to be used in the learning process are a key issue in the development of AI systems.

Depending on the amount of data and the learning method, sooner or later an algorithm will always recognise patterns and use them to make predictions. However, these predictions do not necessarily have to be goal-directed or logical.

It is therefore important that the training data contains the information on which the predictions are based.

In order to make correct predictions from data, the training data must meet several requirements.

Content

As already indicated, the training data used should also provide goal-oriented information, ideally in all conceivable forms.

In terms of the examples, for offboard navigation this means providing the most up-to-date map data possible, traffic guidance information, current and statistical traffic density data, news about road works or closures, but also the occupancy rates of car parks or multi-storey car parks.

In the example of object recognition, data with as many object examples as possible should of course be provided.

Characteristics

In both examples, the characteristics of the information can vary considerably.

While maps are essentially standardised, they can typically vary in terms of the level of detail or scale. Traffic density information, congestion reports, etc. are much more diverse, as there are different sources and therefore different formats for this data.

Overall, the characteristics in this example are still relatively clear.

The consideration of the object recognition example becomes much more complex. The first step is to identify which objects are to be recognised.

If you look at traffic signs, for example, there is already a considerable variety.

Not only are traffic signs country-specific in selection, condition and shape, but positioning, alignment and mounting heights are also variable.

If obstacles can be recognised, the variance increases. This is not only a matter of distinguishing between animate and inanimate obstacles, but also of recognising people of different skin colours, sizes, clothing, hairstyles, accompanying objects, etc., of regionally varying fauna or, in the case of objects, their size or crossability.

Of course, the variance of the underlying image information, light, weather or other disturbances must also be taken into account, or their effects minimised.

The permutations from all the described characteristics virtually force an unbelievable amount of training data.

A smart reduction of the characteristics is therefore urgently required in view of the possible computational performance.

Therefore, in the example of object recognition with obstacle orientation, it would perhaps be more appropriate to reverse the idea, i.e. to recognise lanes free of obstacles.

Safety and ethics

Taking object recognition as an example, there is a clear safety reference to people as obstacles and therefore potential victims.

Therefore, no aspect of human recognition can be ignored. All possible ethnicities, ages, disabilities, means of transport or other objects that can be carried must not lead to a reduction in the prediction rate.

However, the selection of training data is an engineering process that must be done manually. This also means that personal experience - and perhaps not necessarily intentional - as well as preferences come into the process.

This is a major challenge for safety-critical applications and requires a process that is as comprehensive as possible.

3.4. Development training system

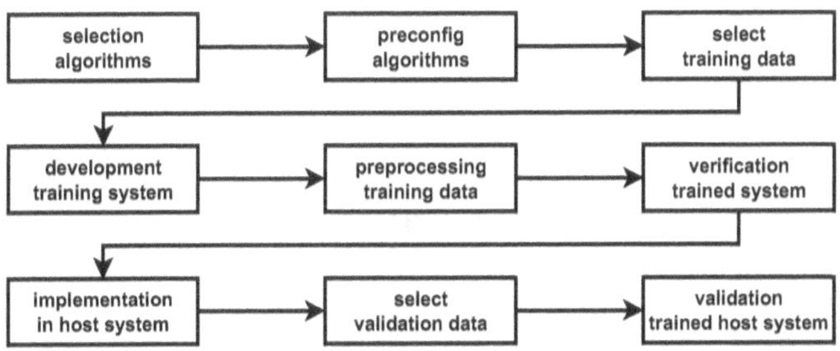

Fig. 3.4.: Development training system

The path from pre-configuration to a trained system requires a suitable environment. This needs two components, a platform for the AI algorithms and an environment that iteratively adjusts the hyperparameters towards the desired goal.

AI platform

A platform is required to run the AI algorithms. Depending on the application, different types of platform are conceivable. Depending on the learning method, the use of this platform is possible for both training and the actual target application.

Regardless of whether training or target application, the algorithm runs as a software application on a hardware platform.

Typical platforms are:

- mainframes[9]
- personal computers
- embedded systems[10], System on Chips (SoCs)
- specific AI Edge Devices
  - GPUs[11]
  - field-programmable gate arrays (FPGAs)
  - dedicated AI accelerators

The platforms essentially differ in terms of:

- processing performance
- amount of data they can handle[12]
- usability for mobile applications
- energy consumptions
- unit costs

Apart from the target application[13], the algorithms are platform-independent, which plays an important role for learning aspects. In this way, it is partly possible to carry out the learning process on high-performance platforms.

However, it is important to remember that the code of the algorithms[14] are executed in an operating system and that there may be fundamentally different software architectures, e.g. embedded OS on the target hardware vs. Linux on the training hardware.

A detailed consideration of these aspects may be necessary in terms of the requirements of functional safety[15].

---

9   e.g. offboard navigation
10   e.g. object recognition
11   e.g. NVIDIA ADAS
12   RAM, storage, data throughput
13   e.g. real-time applications
14   e.g. library with API
15   Software tool criteria evaluation report [38, 11.5.1],
     Software tool qualification report [38, 11.5.2]

Training framework

The purpose of this platform is to feed the training algorithm with training data and iteratively determine the prediction and compare it to the target values by varying and optimising the hyperparameters.

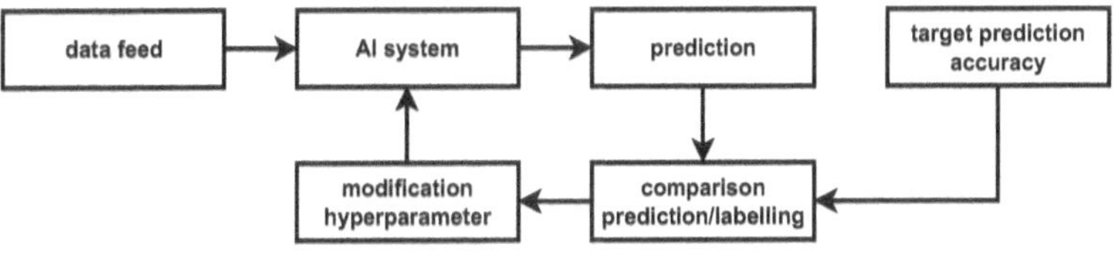

Fig. 3.5.: Training System

The training framework and the AI platform can also be included in the same tool.

Typical frameworks are:

- AI Development Platform
- Machine Learning Framework
- Deep Learning Framework
- AI/ML platform as a service (PaaS)

Again, a detailed consideration may be necessary in terms of the requirements of functional safety[15].

3.5. Preprocessing training data

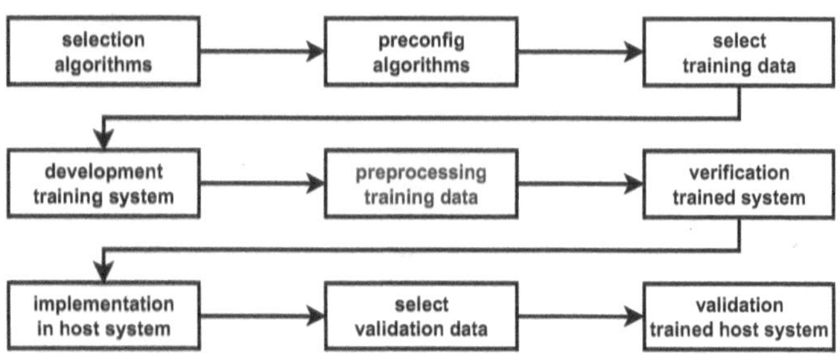

Fig. 3.6.: Preprocessing Training Data

In supervised learning applications, processing the training data is a crucial step.

For instance, in the case of object recognition, the training data typically consists of images or video frames, each of which must be annotated to indicate whether or not it contains the object of interest. This step, referred to as *labelling* or *tagging*, involves manually tagging the data with labels that correspond to the objects being recognized.

The labelling process is vital for the performance of the model, as it defines the ground truth that the algorithm will learn from.

However, this manual process is often highly **time-consuming** and requires a significant level of **accuracy** and **consistency**.

Even small errors or inconsistencies in labelling can have a significant impact on the performance of the trained model, as the algorithm will learn from these flawed labels.

Consequently, inaccuracies in this task will negatively affect the accuracy of the predictions made by the model during its
 deployment.

To further improve the reliability of the labelled data, advanced techniques such as *semi-supervised learning* or *active learning* may be employed, where the model itself can assist in the labelling process or reduce the amount of manual labelling required.

However, even with these techniques, ensuring high-quality labelled data remains one of the most challenging aspects of training a supervised learning model.

3.6. Verification trained system

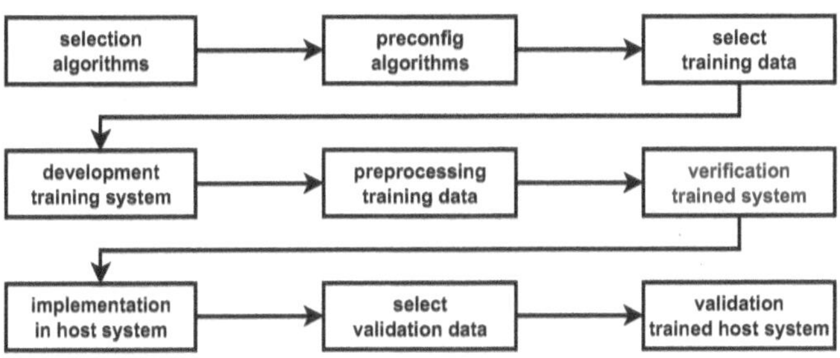

Fig. 3.7.: Verification trained system

Software development also includes the right branch of the V model, namely verification and validation, which play a crucial role in ensuring the correctness and reliability of the system.

In the context of machine learning, to check the accuracy of the predictions made by the trained algorithm, it is essential to conduct test runs with data that the algorithm has not seen during its training phase.

These *test data sets* allow for an unbiased evaluation of the model's generalization ability, i.e., how well it performs on new, unseen data. This process is often referred to as *model evaluation* or *testing*. This step is not to be confused with the validation step.

However, it is important to note that the same quality standards applied to the training data must also be enforced on the verification (test) data sets. Just as the model's performance depends on the quality of the training data, the accuracy of the predictions is highly sensitive to the integrity and relevance of the verification data.

Poor-quality or incorrectly labelled verification data can lead to misleading results and an inaccurate assessment of the model's true performance.

Thus, ensuring the consistency, correctness, and representativeness of the test data is as critical as preparing the training data itself. Only by applying rigorous quality control to both training and verification datasets can we ensure that the model's predictions are reliable and accurate.

3.7. Implementation AI application in host system

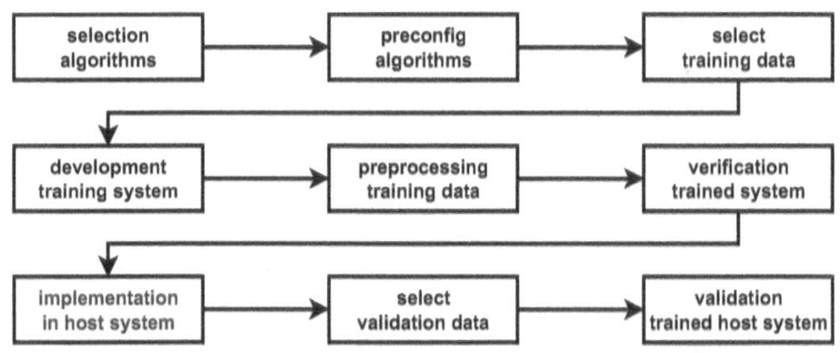

Fig. 3.8.: Implementation in Host System

An AI algorithm is not stand-alone and cannot be used in isolation; therefore, its implementation within a *host system* is necessary.

The host system provides the necessary infrastructure, interfaces, and resources to enable the AI algorithm to function in real-world applications, ensuring it can process data, interact with other system components, and meet operational requirements.

Safety-critical functions, as defined by ISO 26262, are typically characterised by high availability and latency requirements. AI-based applications must meet these requirements.

Web-based functions do not currently meet these requirements, so only on-board applications can be used in this context.

The development of AI host systems is particularly interesting when they are used in safety-related applications and can be assigned safety goals.

3.7.1. Hardware

Off-board AI systems are currently conceivable in the automotive world wherever particularly large amounts of data from a wide variety of sources need to be processed. Examples include navigation tasks such as time-uncritical route calculation, advertising or multimedia applications.

Due to the sheer volume of data from different sources and the potential number of users, AI applications are much more likely to be found in server farms than locally in the vehicle. In the applications mentioned, the vehicle functions only as an operating and display device, i.e. Human Machine Interface (HMI).

Due to the unpredictability of wireless internet connectivity for off-board systems[16], on-board systems[17] are more likely

---

[16] The controls or algorithms required to perform the function are not executed locally in the vehicle, but on servers at the OEM or service provider.

[17] The controls or algorithms required to perform the function are executed locally in the vehicle. There is no need for computation on servers at OEMs or service providers.

to be used for safety-related applications. For on-board systems, aspects such as power consumption and unit price are important decision criteria for the selection of suitable hardware platforms.

Looking at the AI platform section, embedded systems are therefore the first choice here.

Irrespective of the processor architectures used, hardware platform development is a classic Electronic Control Unit (ECU) development that must be carried out according to Part 5 of ISO 26262 for safety-related applications.

This ISO 26262 may not yet be fully prepared for AI specific hardware. Hardware design, for all its complexity, is a well-known topic and, except for component selection, hardly AI specific.

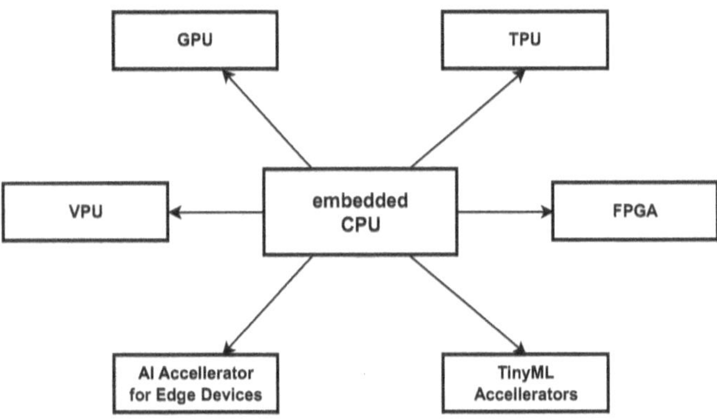

Fig. 3.9.: AI specific hardware

Embedded systems, particularly those implementing artificial intelligence at the edge, require specialized hardware to handle the processing demands of AI models.

These hardware components are optimized for specific tasks, such as deep learning, image recognition, and real-time processing, and offer low power consumption and high performance.

Below is a summary of the key AI hardware components:

GRAPHICS PROCESSING UNITS (GPUs) are widely used for parallel processing tasks and are ideal for deep learning applications due to their ability to handle large-scale data processing simultaneously. They are particularly suited for high-demand AI tasks, such as image classification and neural network training.

FIELD-PROGRAMMABLE GATE ARRAYS (FPGAs) are programmable chips that allow developers to optimize the hardware for specific AI tasks. They are commonly used in embedded systems due to their flexibility, low power consumption, and high-performance capabilities for edge AI applications.

TENSOR PROCESSING UNITS (TPUs) are specialized hardware accelerators designed for deep learning tasks developed by Google. They provide highly efficient processing for matrix operations, commonly used in AI models such as neural networks. TPUs are particularly suited for real-time AI processing.

VISION PROCESSING UNITS (VPUs) are optimized for computer vision tasks and are essential for applications such as autonomous vehicles and surveillance systems. They provide high efficiency in processing visual data such as images and video streams.

EDGE AI ACCELERATORS are designed for low-power, real-time AI processing on edge devices, such as IoT devices and wearables. They reduce latency by processing AI tasks directly on the device without the need for cloud communication.

TINYML ACCELERATORS designed for small, low-power devices, TinyML accelerators enable AI inference in constrained environments, such as smart home devices, sensors, and health monitors. These accelerators allow for real-time processing with minimal energy usage.

These specialized AI hardware components enable embedded systems to efficiently run AI models in real-time while managing power and space constraints, which is crucial for applications such as autonomous systems, IoT, and edge computing.

3.7.2. Software

As already written above, I limit myself to on-board systems when considering the implementation of AI.

There are many different ways of implementing AI in ECU software, depending on, among other things, constellations of distributed development.

The local execution of the prediction is done by parametrised algorithms of the nodes. This offers the possibility of different implementation methods.

The fig. 3.10 shows two implementation options in embedded environments using AUTomotive Open System ARchitecture (AUTOSAR) Classic Platform as an example. The figure shows two different implementations, which differ in principle only in that the AI components are encapsulated either directly in the Software Component (SWC) or in a library.

Of course, other implementations are possible, for example with AI parameters outsourced from the SWC, which could provide advantages in software release and partial flashing. However, this has no significant impact on the considerations.

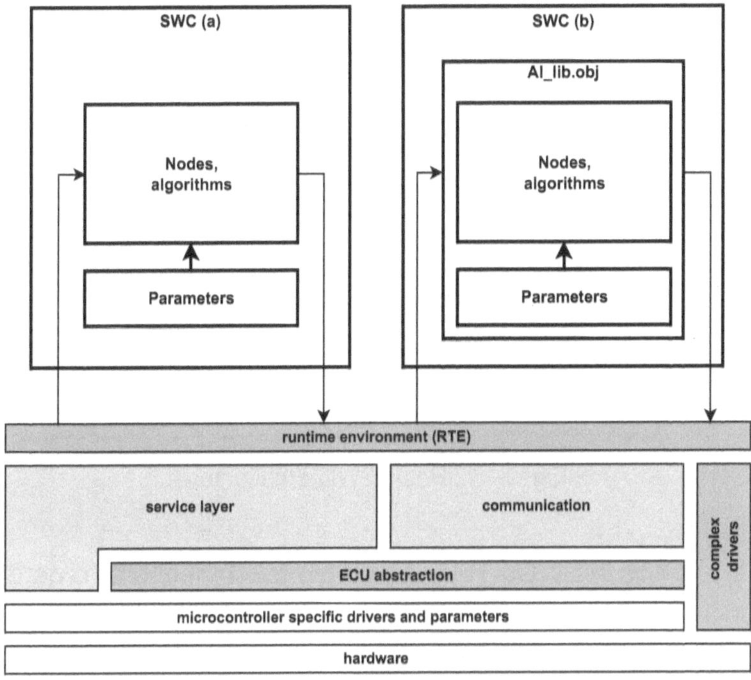

Fig. 3.10.: AI SWCs implementation in AUTOSAR

An implementation in AUTOSAR Adaptive Platform [2] differs essentially only in the interfaces provided to the SWC. The basic concept of the SWC is not significantly different.

Comparing the implementation of classic automotive functionalities with AI-based functions, no real differences can be observed.

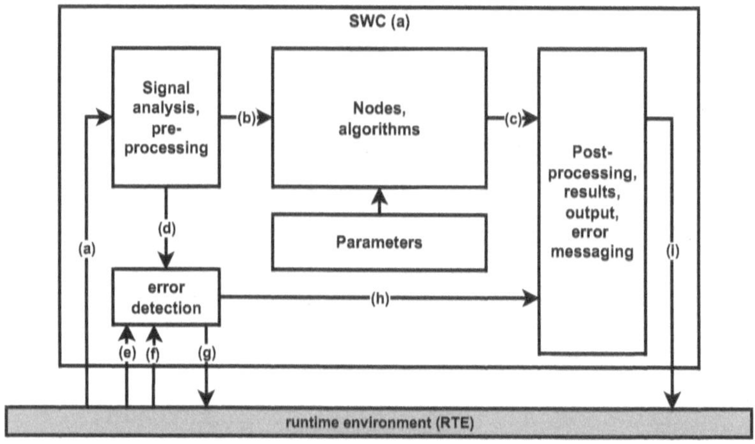

Fig. 3.11.: Basic SWC architecture

If you look in SWCs, you will find typical components regardless of their functionality. These are briefly described below.

Of course, other architectures are also possible, e.g. by executing the components described below as separate SWCs. The resulting flows, shown as arrows, remain.

Signal analysis, Pre-processing

Typically, the input data (a) required for the execution of the functionality is checked for various criteria.

- availability
- actuality

- integrity[18]
- validity[19]

- plausibility
- security

Depending on the application, the input data may be passed to the function (b) without further processing, or it may be corrected. Any indication that the input data is faulty is passed (d) on to the error detection module.

---

[18]   e.g. E2E
[19]   e.g. value ranges, gradient monitoring, failure bands

In addition, the provision of positive and negative sample patterns could be implemented as a start-up test, in the sense of a self-diagnosis of the functioning of the neural networks.

Functional algorithm (e.g. AI)

The 'Nodes, Algorithms' module is an example of all possible functionalities and does not differ from classical functions. Outputs (c) are generated from input data (b) by parameterised algorithms.

Whether the algorithm represents a controller function or an object recognition based on AI is irrelevant.

Parameters

In the context of specific applications, it may be advantageous not to hardcode parameters into the function algorithm.

On the one hand, this allows the algorithm to be released independently of the parameters, and on the other hand, different parameter sets can be easily implemented. Partial (separate) updates are also possible. In this context, Over The Air (OTA) updates should also be mentioned.

On the other hand, algorithms with infrequently adjusted parameters and special attention to high processing speed and memory optimisation can benefit from hardcoded parameters.

Error detection

The error detection module records all errors relevant to the correct execution of the functionality.

These may be transmitted by the signal analyser (d), for example, or by the host system (e, f). Typical errors would be:

- timeouts (d)
- signal failures (d),
  see Signal analysis, Pre-processing
- signal usability[20] (d)
- software failures host system (e)
- hardware failures host system (f)

The 'Error detection' module informs (g) the host system about detected errors for the central error documentation.

Post-processing, result output, error handling

This module can be implemented in a number of ways, depending on the application. As a basic function, it is recommended that the algorithm results are passed (i) to the host system for further use if they are error free.

In the event of an error, several scenarios are possible. For example, the output data could be modified[21] to either eliminate the error or at least reduce its impact.

The output data could also be marked as invalid for certain errors and substitute values could be output.

Alternatively, the output data could be left unchanged, but the user of the data could be informed of a reduced confidence level.

---

[20]   example of an object detection video stream:
too bright, too dark, low contrast (e.g. fog, mist), distortion (e.g. raindrops).

[21]   limitation of value range, gradient adjustments

Multiple AI Applications

AI components can be integrated into a Software Component (SWC) in various ways, not just as single elements, but also as complex constructs that incorporate multiple AI modules with different functionalities.

These configurations can enable the system to handle more sophisticated tasks, leveraging the strengths of each AI component to complement one another. For instance, an SWC could integrate AI-driven components for decision-making, sensory data interpretation, and predictive maintenance, all working together to achieve a broader range of goals.

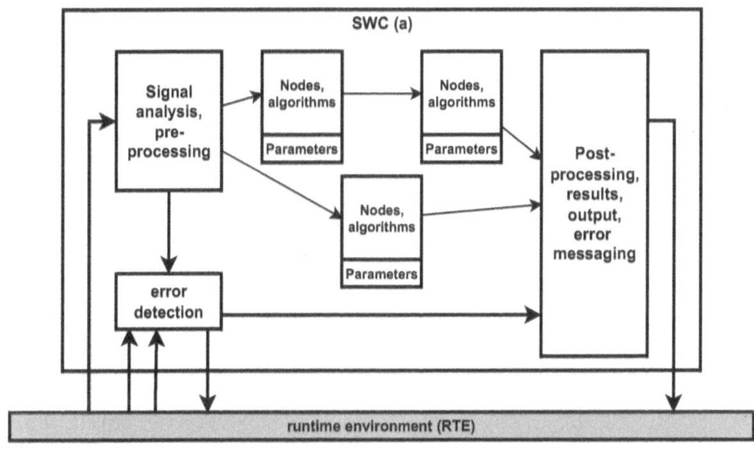

Fig. 3.12.: Implementation of Multiple AI Applications

Despite the complexity introduced by using multiple AI components, this approach does not fundamentally alter the core principles of AI development.

The integration remains rooted in established AI methodologies, with each component still adhering to the overall software architecture and functional requirements of the system.

The challenge lies in ensuring smooth interaction and seamless communication between the different AI modules, maintaining the robustness and reliability of the system while harnessing the power of multiple AI technologies.

3.8. Selection Validation Data

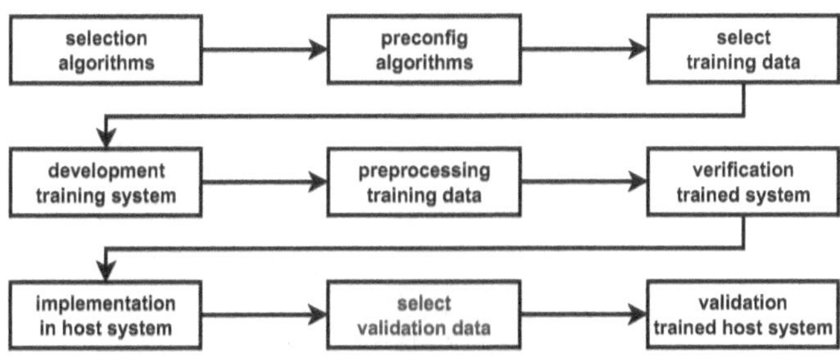

Fig. 3.13.: Selection Validation Data

When selecting appropriate validation data for AI applications, it is essential to ensure that the data used for validation is of the highest quality and distinct from the training data.

One such concept is the use of 'golden samples', which refers to a set of validation data that has been carefully curated and not used in the training process.

Golden samples serve as a reliable benchmark for evaluating the performance of the trained model, as they represent high-quality, real-world data that the model has not previously encountered.

The quality of the validation data is paramount. Not only must the data be representative of the conditions the model will encounter in production, but it must also undergo rigorous *labelling*.

This means that the labels assigned to the validation data should be accurate and consistent, reflecting the true characteristics of the data. The labelling process must adhere to strict quality standards to avoid errors that could lead to misleading validation results and, in turn, a false sense of model performance.

3.9. Validation trained Host System

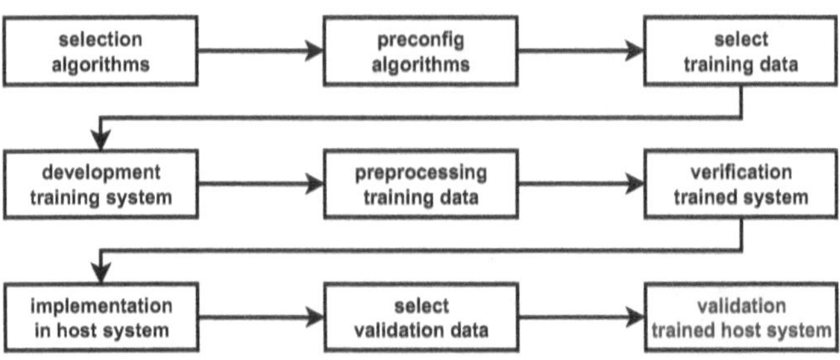

Fig. 3.14.: Validation trained host system

Validation within the *host system* goes beyond assessing the prediction accuracy of the AI model. In addition to assessing the prediction rate, it is essential to examine the overall performance of the host system itself.

This includes ensuring that the system can handle the computational load required by the AI application, particularly in terms of processing speed, memory usage and resource allocation. The host system must be capable of efficiently executing the AI model under real-world conditions, ensuring that the system operates within the defined performance parameters, such as latency and throughput.

Validation in the host system also involves verifying that the AI application meets the expectations of the end user. This includes ensuring that the AI system delivers outputs that are consistent with user requirements and desired outcomes.

The validation process must confirm that the application works as intended in its operational environment and provides the user with results that are accurate, reliable and actionable. This step is critical to ensure that the AI application fulfils its intended purpose and meets user satisfaction, both in terms of performance and usability.

4. Summary terms and technical background

In 'Purpose and Technical Basis of Electronic Systems' p. 4 the basic functions of electronic systems were explained, which are crucial for modern technological applications. These systems are designed to perform tasks such as control, regulation, communication, display and user interaction.

Their versatility is evident in areas such as automotive, industrial automation and aerospace.

Particular emphasis is placed on control mechanisms, including feedback loops and signal processing, which can be enhanced through the integration of artificial intelligence (AI).

By incorporating AI, these systems promise to become more adaptive and intelligent, capable of responding to complex and dynamic environments.

The foundations have been laid for understanding how classical control techniques and AI can complement each other to improve efficiency and flexibility.

'Artifical Intelligence' p. 12 and the following chapters discuss the most important concepts of AI and machine learning.

Artificial intelligence is essentially a software-based technology that can make predictions from input data by learning parameterised algorithms.

The accuracy of the prediction depends on several aspects, including

- learning method
- choice and accuracy of algorithms
- number of nodes in the network
- precision of the learning goal definition
- usefulness of the training data
- sufficient training environment
- usefulness of training interations
- usefulness of the input data
- performance of the host system

⚙ processes, 🔧 tools, 🛢 training data, 👁 sensor data, ☷ host system

There are two main concepts for automotive AI applications: offboard and onboard.

In offboard applications, the car serves only as a control and display device, which is familiar territory in automotive electronics. For safety-related applications with real-time requirements and high availability, onboard applications are (currently) the best choice.

For largely reproducible prediction results in combination with embedded systems, supervised learning is the most suitable method.

In the control unit, an AI component is implemented as **statically programmed algorithms** with equally **static parameters**, analogous to conventional functions.

Machine Learning therefore only takes place during the development of the application, and **not in the ECU**. It is only the neural network that is active in the control unit.

I see the core issues for safety-relevant applications as primarily process and tool issues.

5. Application AI in technical applications

The objective of this section is to provide an overview of AI use cases in **relation to technical solutions**, highlighting how artificial intelligence can address specific challenges and contribute to innovative advancements in various applications.

Although the focus is on automotive applications, derivatives are possible for other technical applications such as medical, agricultural, IoT, leisure or industrial systems.

Applications related to processes will be discussed in the following parts.

5.1. Application in Functions

In this section we will explore various applications of AI in different functional areas, focusing on both the more obvious and less obvious use cases.

The examples, which can certainly be extended, are intended to illustrate how AI can be used to enhance the performance and capabilities of systems in a range of domains.

This general overview will provide insights into the potential for further development and application of AI in these functions.

Part II p. 88 and following will provide a more detailed insight.

5.1.1. Customer Function

One of the most obvious areas where AI can be applied is in enhancing the customer experience. AI systems are already being used in several ways to improve the interaction between customers and their vehicles, as well as to optimize various vehicle functions for **convenience**, **safety**, and **efficiency**.

ROUTE PLANNING FOR NAVIGATION SYSTEMS AI plays a key role in **route planning** for modern navigation systems. By analysing real-time traffic data, weather conditions and road closures, AI can optimise routes, reducing time and fuel consumption.

In addition, predictive models can anticipate potential delays and suggest alternative routes, providing a seamless driving experience for the customer.

Systems such as Google Maps and Waze, for example, use machine learning algorithms to adjust routes based on real-time data, improving accuracy and efficiency.

OBJECT DETECTION Object recognition is a critical aspect of advanced driver assistance systems. AI-based object recognition systems can **detect and classify objects** in the environment, such as traffic signs, obstacles, pedestrians, vehicles and road markings.

This capability is essential for Advanced Driver Assistance Systems (ADAS), which support functions such as traffic sign recognition, road condition monitoring, and even **driver and occupant monitoring**.

For example, AI-based traffic sign recognition systems can automatically detect and interpret traffic signs, alerting the driver to changes in speed limits, stop signs and other important road information.

Similarly, occupant monitoring systems use cameras and machine learning to **detect driver attention levels** and warn of potential fatigue or distraction.

TRAJECTORY PREDICTION FOR AUTONOMOUS DRIVING
Trajectory prediction is a critical component of autonomous driving technology. AI algorithms analyse the movement of surrounding objects and predict their future positions, helping autonomous vehicles to make safe and informed driving decisions.

By combining data from cameras, radar and lidar sensors, AI models can **calculate and optimise the trajectory** of vehicles including the ego vehicle, pedestrians and cyclists in real time, ensuring that the autonomous vehicle can navigate safely and efficiently.

ENERGY CONSUMPTION PLANNING AND PREDICTION In the context of Electric Vehicle (EV), AI can be used for energy planning and prediction.

By analysing historical driving patterns, road types and environmental conditions, AI systems can **estimate remaining battery life** and **suggest optimal charging strategies**.

These systems can also help manufacturers design more energy-efficient vehicles by predicting energy requirements at different stages of a journey.

PLAUSIBILITY CHECKS AI can improve both safety and security by performing plausibility checks in driving situations.

By analysing the context of a driving scenario, AI can **detect anomalous or unsafe behaviour**, such as erratic lane changes or sudden stops, and **alert the driver or intervene** if necessary.

In addition, AI can help **protect against cybersecurity threats** by continuously monitoring for unusual patterns of behaviour, such as unauthorised access attempts or tampering with vehicle systems.

5.1.2. System Function

In contrast to customer-facing applications, there are less obvious but equally important use cases for AI within the internal systems of vehicles. These applications focus on improving the reliability, performance and safety of complex vehicle systems.

WEAR AND TEAR ANALYSIS   One of the key system functions where AI can be applied is wear and tear analysis.

By continuously **monitoring the condition of critical components** such as the engine, brakes or tyres, AI can **detect early signs of deterioration** and predict when maintenance or replacement will be required.

Predictive maintenance, powered by machine learning models, helps reduce downtime and extend the life of vehicle components by scheduling maintenance activities before they lead to costly failures.

FAULT CONDITION DETECTION AND TREND ANALYSIS   AI can also be used to **detect fault conditions in very complex vehicle systems** with numerous variants, variables and even more unknowns.

By **consolidating and analysing data** from sensors and on-board diagnostic tools, AI systems can identify patterns that indicate faults or degradation in various vehicle subsystems, such as the transmission, electrical systems or cooling mechanisms.

Trend analysis using machine learning models enables the system to detect early-stage faults that may not be visible to traditional diagnostic tools, enabling faster intervention and reducing the risk of unexpected breakdowns.

IN-CAR CYBERSECURITY FORENSICS   As vehicles become increasingly connected, ensuring their cybersecurity has become a top priority.

On-board AI systems can help **monitor and analyse network traffic**, **detect intrusions and perform forensics** in the event of a cyber attack.

AI-powered systems can **identify suspicious activity**, such as **unauthorised access attempts**, tampering with control systems or malicious data transfers.

These systems can then respond in real time by isolating compromised components or alerting security teams to prevent further damage.   Methods from the IT world can be transferred to the vehicle system.

ACCIDENT DATA STORAGE   Another critical system function enhanced by AI is the storage and analysis of accident data.

The complexity of driving situations, sensor data, external information and potential attack vectors leads to an overwhelming number of accident causes when considered in permutations.

As the amount of data generated by sensors and system communication increases, so do the storage requirements.

The aim is to use AI to **identify and record accident-prone situations**, ensuring that sufficient data sets are available for further analysis, while **filtering out irrelevant information** at an early stage. Relevant data is then prioritised for future investigation.

In the event of a crash, AI can automatically record and securely store critical data such as vehicle speed, braking patterns and sensor readings in a tamper-proof manner.

This data is invaluable for post-crash analysis, helping investigators understand accident causes and refine safety protocols or cybersecurity measures.

In addition, AI can assist in accident reconstruction by analysing multiple data sources to create a detailed account of the event, contributing to improved vehicle safety design.

5.2. Process Support for Product Lifecycle

Artificial intelligence (AI) has become a transformative force across industries, offering unparalleled opportunities to optimise and innovate throughout the entire product lifecycle.

The advancements in AI are reshaping how businesses approach design, production, and maintenance, leading to smarter, more efficient processes and products.

From the earliest stages of conceptual design and engineering through to manufacturing, deployment, and eventual decommissioning, AI technologies can be leveraged to address specific challenges and unlock value at each stage.

By enabling more informed decisions, automating repetitive tasks, and offering deeper insights into data, AI can drastically enhance productivity and product quality while ensuring better resource allocation.

The application of AI enables improved decision-making, predictive analytics, and process automation, which together enhance efficiency, reduce operational costs, and promote sustainability in various sectors.

Through intelligent forecasting, better risk management, and optimized workflows, AI helps businesses streamline their operations and stay competitive.

This section explores the specific roles and benefits of AI at different stages of the product lifecycle, highlighting the various aspects that come into play depending on the phase and context.

By examining the ways AI contributes to each stage, from early design decisions to post-deployment maintenance and decommissioning, we gain a deeper understanding of how this technology can drive continuous improvement, reduce downtime, and enhance the overall performance and sustainability of products.

Following an initial overview of the product lifecycle.

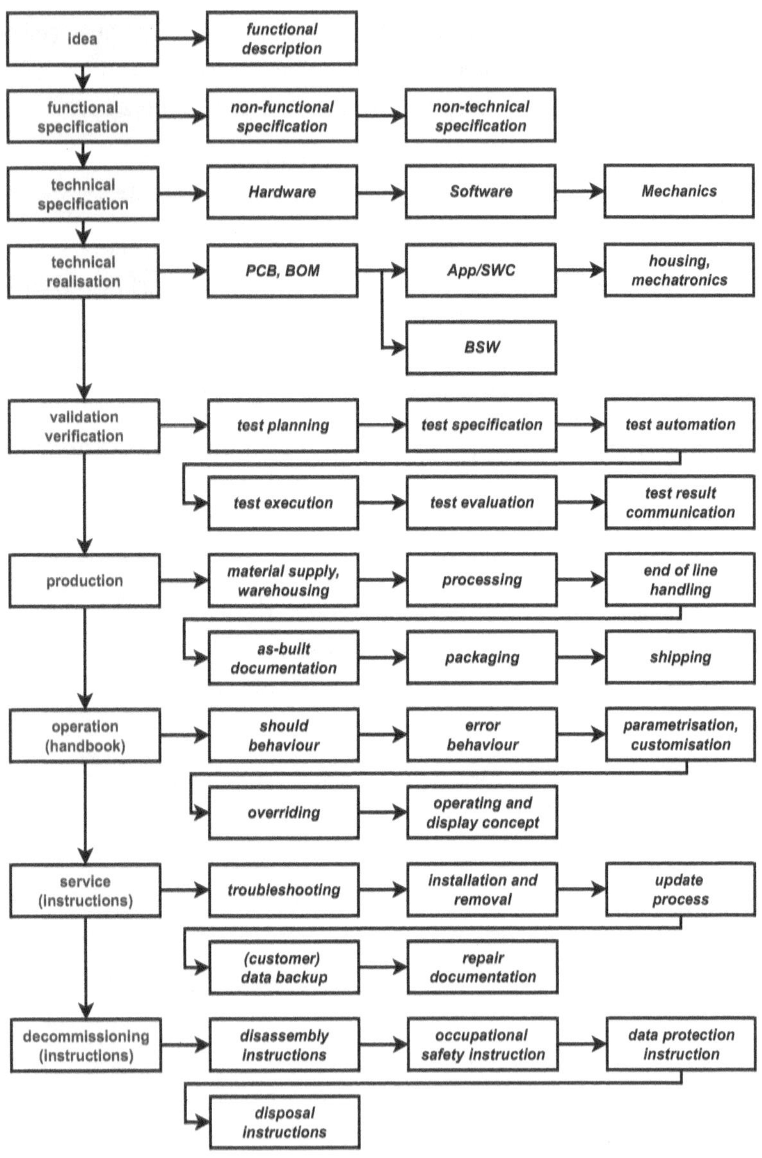

Fig. 5.1.: Product Life Cycle (PLC)

5.2.1. Idea

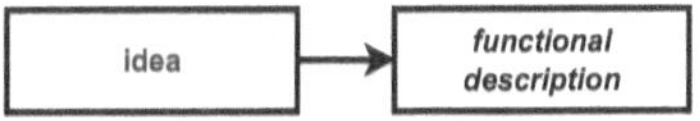

Fig. 5.2.: PLC - Idea

AI offers significant potential to support the idea-making phase by improving the process of documenting and refining the idea description.

For example, AI systems can automatically draft **functional description** [25] based on input data or templates, streamlining the initial stages of documentation.

In addition, machine learning algorithms can assess the completeness of an idea by cross-referencing it with existing databases or knowledge repositories, identifying overlooked aspects or gaps early in the process.

Initial market analyses can also be easily taken over and carried out by AI, assuming clever prompting.

This ensures that the foundation of the project is both robust and well-rounded.

5.2.2. Functional Specification

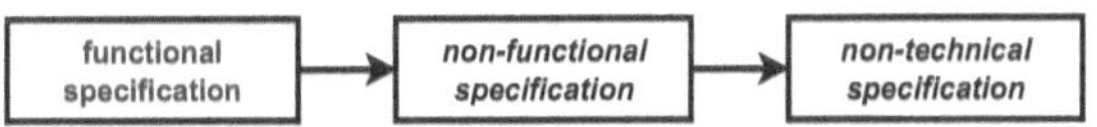

Fig. 5.3.: PLC - Functional Specification

In the functional specification phase, AI can play an important role in ensuring that the functional requirements are seamlessly aligned with the original idea.

Natural Language Processing (NLP) algorithms can **analyse requirements** documents for clarity, coherence and consistency, highlighting ambiguities or inconsistencies.

AI tools can also support compliance with requirements engineering principles such as atomicity and testability by breaking down complex requirements into simpler, more actionable elements. In addition, AI-powered **review** systems can identify inconsistencies or missing elements and provide recommendations for improvement.

During audits or assessments, AI systems can automate compliance checks, ensuring that the specification is in line with industry standards and best practices.

AI can analyse not only functional specifications, but also **non-functional specifications** and **non-technical specifications** from different sources.

AI-driven tools can automate the analysis of standards and referenced documents, ensuring that no critical policy or requirement is overlooked.

Using NLP and data mining techniques, these systems can assess the relevance and applicability of standards to the project context and perform detailed gap analysis where necessary.

For example, AI can identify areas where current documents are outdated or incomplete, and suggest updates based on recent regulatory changes.

In addition, AI can extract and formulate technical requirements from complex legal or normative texts, significantly reducing the manual effort involved in this task.

5.2.3. Technical Specification

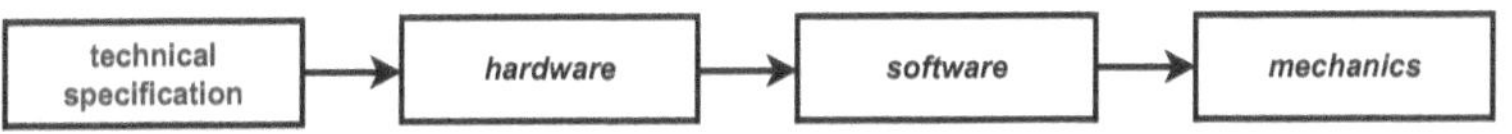

Fig. 5.4.: PLC - Technical Specification

The technical specification phase benefits greatly from AI's ability to establish and maintain traceability between different specification levels.

Using advanced graph-based models, AI can map the relationships between the functional, non-functional and technical specifications, ensuring coherence across all levels as well as between **hardware**, **software** and **mechanics**.

The oversimplified example in fig. 5.5 shows how complex the alignment between the different specifications can be.

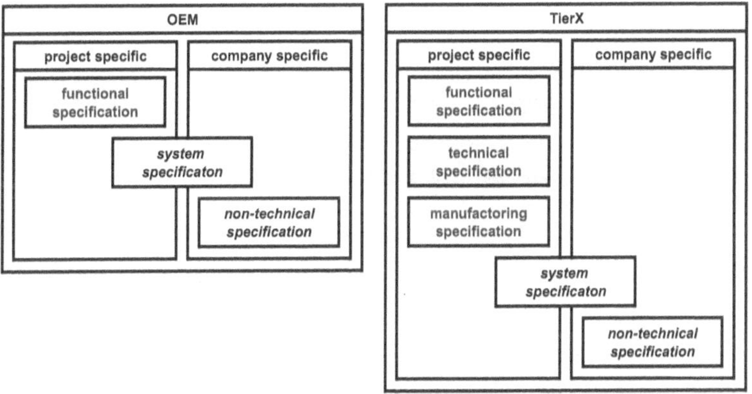

Fig. 5.5.: Alignment Specifications

Machine learning can also validate compliance with requirements engineering principles by analysing the text for clarity and consistency.

During **reviews**, AI systems can provide guidance and insights into potential weaknesses, such as overly complex wording or omitted details.

During audits, automated tools can compare the specification against pre-defined standards to identify deviations.

In addition, AI can facilitate the alignment of technical specifications with other domains, such as hardware or software, by simulating the interactions between these components.

5.2.4. Technical Realisation

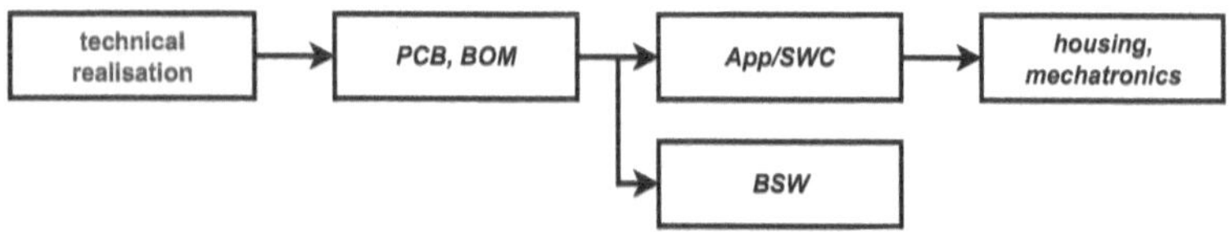

Fig. 5.6.: PLC - Technical Realisation

Throughout the technical realisation phase, AI systems can automate the **creation** and **management** of technical documentation, ensuring accuracy and completeness, as well as **tool-based technical solutions**.

In bug tracking, predictive analytics powered by machine learning can help **prioritise issues** by assessing their **potential impact** on the project schedule or quality.

For project management, AI tools can predict risks, optimise resource allocation and monitor progress in real time, providing valuable insights for decision making.

AI can also integrate with version control systems to track development progress, identify potential deviations from the planned schedule and suggest corrective actions to keep the project on track.

5.2.5. Verification and validation

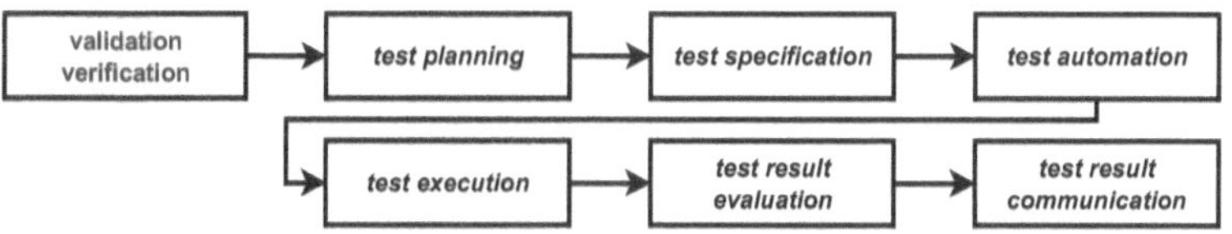

Fig. 5.7.: PLC - Verification and validation

In the context of AI, verification and validation (V&V) play a critical role in ensuring that AI systems are reliable, accurate, and perform as expected in real-world environments. The following sections discuss the application potentials of AI in the V&V process, focusing on different stages of testing.

TEST PLANNING   Test planning is an essential phase in the verification and validation process, determining the **scope**, **approach**, and **resources** needed for testing an AI system. AI technologies can enhance test planning by analyzing historical test data to predict areas with high risk or complexity.

Machine learning algorithms can also help **prioritize test cases**, ensuring that limited resources are allocated to the most critical parts of the system. Furthermore, AI can assist in optimizing **test coverage** by identifying test scenarios that have not been sufficiently explored.

An important aspect of test planning is **ensuring compliance** with relevant safety and security standards. AI can support this by automatically cross-referencing test requirements with applicable standards, flagging any areas where compliance may be lacking, and suggesting additional tests to address safety-critical requirements.

TEST SPECIFICATION   Automated test specification generation involves defining the inputs, expected outputs and execution steps for each test case.

AI can automate this process by learning from the behaviour of the system and generating test specifications that reflect the functional requirements of the system.

Traceability to the underlying specifications is also ensured.

NLP techniques can be employed to derive test specifications from high-level requirements or documentation, while reinforcement learning models can be used to simulate various edge cases and generate corresponding test scenarios.

AUTOMATED TEST CASE PROGRAMMING   Automating **test case programming** helps speed up the testing process by generating and executing test cases without manual intervention.

AI can be used to automatically generate test scripts based on system behavior, usage patterns, or code changes. For example, AI-driven test case generation tools can analyze the structure of the software and create a suite of test cases that comprehensively cover the codebase.

Moreover, AI can **adapt and improve the test cases** over time by learning from past test executions, ensuring that new tests are always relevant and effective.

TEST CAMPAIGN EXECUTION   Test campaign[1] execution in AI systems can be optimised by taking into account feature planning and the current implementation status of the system.

AI can dynamically select which tests to run based on which features are being developed or changed, reducing unnecessary testing effort.

In addition, AI systems can prioritise test execution based on the most critical areas of the system, ensuring that the most important components are validated first.

---

[1]   collection of test cases for a defined test execution

This approach can significantly reduce testing time while improving the efficiency and coverage of the testing process.

TEST RESULT EVALUATION Test result evaluation is the process of analysing the results of executed tests to determine whether the tested system is behaving as expected.

AI can assist in this phase by automating the analysis of test results, comparing observed behaviour with expected outcomes, and detecting discrepancies[2].

Machine learning models can also identify patterns in test results, allowing better prediction of future system behaviour. This enables faster identification and resolution of issues, making the overall testing process more efficient and effective.

TEST RESULT COMMUNICATION Once test results have been analysed, it is vital to communicate them effectively to stakeholders.

AI can automate the generation of detailed, easy-to-understand reports that summarise test results and highlight potential issues. In addition, AI-powered tools can prioritise test results to ensure that the most critical issues are addressed first.

NLP techniques can be used to generate written summaries that provide clear explanations of test results, making it easier for non-technical stakeholders to understand the results and take appropriate action.

---

[2] exclusion of defects from test specification, test case programming or defects based on test equipment

5.2.6. Production

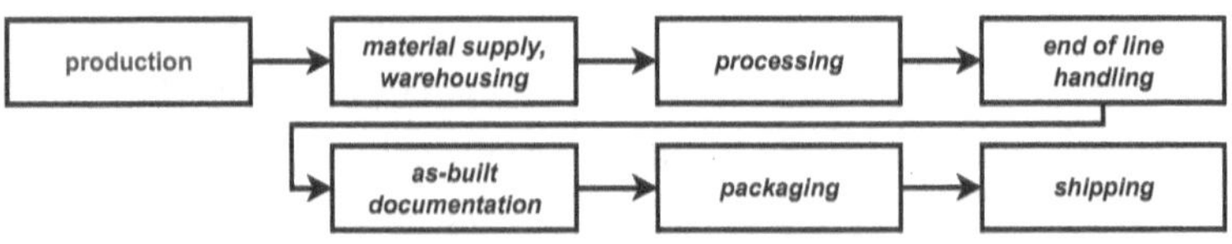

Fig. 5.8.: PLC - Production

At the production stage, AI can **optimise the handling of components** by thoroughly analysing the bill of materials, cross-referencing it with associated manuals, and incorporating manufacturers' recommendations to ensure maximum efficiency and cost-effectiveness and recommendations following the **safety manuals** [40, Cl.9].

It can continuously monitor production processes in real time, detecting **inefficiencies** and identifying potential issues before they escalate.

AI can also track **deviations**, **wear**, and **damage** to production equipment, offering valuable insights that allow for early intervention. Furthermore, it can **recommend adjustments** to improve both productivity and product quality, facilitating smoother operations and reducing downtime.

With the use of predictive analytics, AI can help **identify critical paths and bottlenecks** in the production process, enabling timely, proactive measures to prevent delays or disruptions. By forecasting potential issues, AI provides the opportunity to plan ahead, ensuring a more stable and reliable production flow.

Automated documentation systems, enhanced with AI, are capable of generating detailed and accurate production records with minimal human intervention, ensuring not only consistency but also a high level of precision. This reduces the risk of human error and ensures compliance with regulatory standards, leading to better overall quality control.

5.2.7. Operation

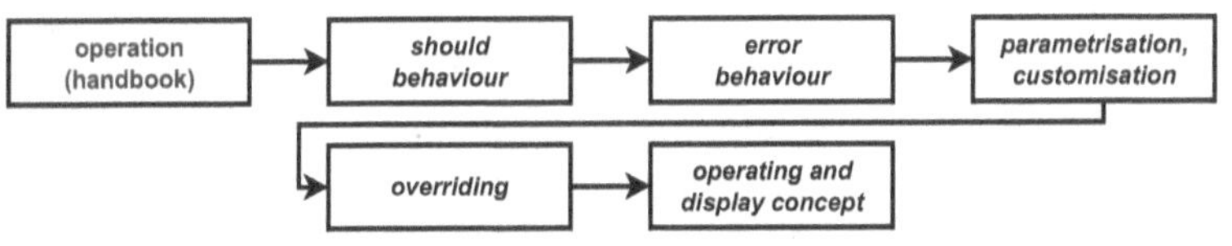

Fig. 5.9.: PLC - Operation

Natural Language Generation (NLG) systems can **improve readability** by producing documentation that is both clear and easy to use.

For international markets, AI-driven **translation** tools ensure that manuals are translated accurately, preserving context and intent.

In addition, AI systems can monitor and verify **compliance with regulatory requirements**, such as homologation standards[3], ensuring that all required documentation meets regulatory expectations.

AI can greatly simplify the **creation of customer manuals** by automatically generating tailored content that aligns with specific product features and addresses the unique needs of users, ensuring that the documentation is both relevant and informative.

NLG systems can significantly **improve readability** by producing documentation that is not only clear and easy to use but also structured in a way that enhances user understanding. This ensures that the end-user can easily navigate and

---

[3]   e.g. ISO 26262

comprehend the manual, reducing the need for extensive support.

Conversions between different media for the operations handbooks are also no problem thanks to AI.

For international markets, AI-driven **translation** tools play a essential role in ensuring that manuals are accurately translated across multiple languages. These systems are capable of preserving both the context and intent of the original content, which is essential for **maintaining consistency** and **preventing misinterpretation** in different linguistic and cultural environments.

In addition to language translation, AI systems can actively monitor and verify **compliance with regulatory requirements**, such as homologation standards[4], ensuring that all necessary documentation adheres to regulatory expectations.

By automating this process, AI can **reduce the risk of non-compliance**, provide real-time updates on regulatory changes, and streamline the approval process, ultimately improving the efficiency of meeting industry standards.

5.2.8. Service

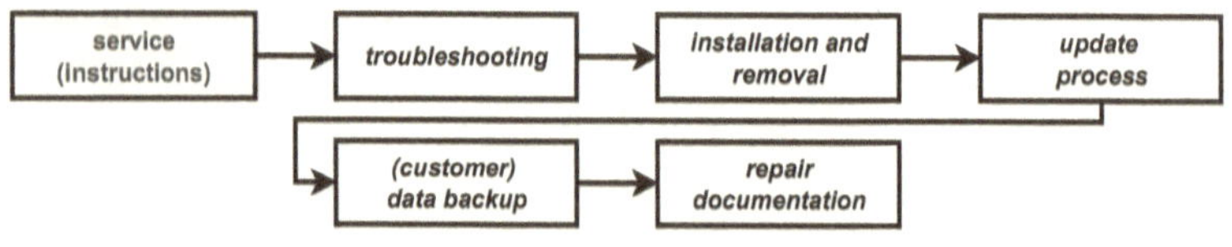

Fig. 5.10.: PLC - Service

AI can revolutionise service processes by developing and optimising intelligent **troubleshooting plans**. These plans can

---

4   e.g. ISO 26262

use historical data and real-time diagnostics to provide step-by-step solutions to resolve problems.

Predictive maintenance systems powered by AI can predict potential failures[5], reducing downtime and improving customer satisfaction.

In addition, AI can assist in the repair process by **suggesting optimal workflows**, identifying required parts and even **guiding technicians** through complex procedures using Augmented Reality (AR) applications.

5.2.9. Decommissioning

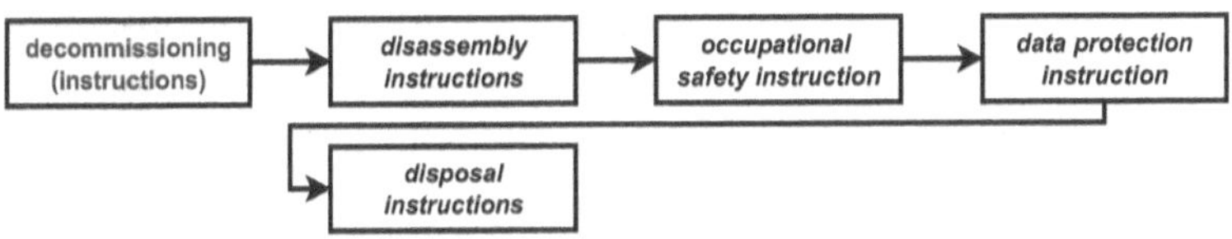

Fig. 5.11.: PLC - Decommissioning

In the decommissioning phase, AI can **generate tailored instructions** to ensure the safe and efficient removal of products from service.

It can **analyse global environmental regulations** to provide up-to-date guidance on disposal and recycling processes, ensuring compliance with country-specific requirements.

AI can also review occupational health and safety standards to create procedures that protect workers during decommissioning.

In addition, AI's ongoing monitoring of regulatory changes ensures that the decommissioning process remains in line with evolving environmental and safety legislation.

---

[5]   the possibility of application errors by service personnel

AI can fully realise its potential, especially when it comes to monitoring regulations.

5.2.10. Summary of Application in Product Life Cycle

Diverse use cases for AI are conceivable and are already being applied in several areas, particularly in the context of production processes and documentation.

AI has the potential to optimize component handling, monitor production processes in real time, and identify inefficiencies or deviations, which helps improve productivity and quality.

Furthermore, AI can automate the generation of tailored customer manuals, enhance readability through NLG systems, and ensure accurate translations for international markets.

It can also monitor compliance with regulatory requirements, such as homologation standards, ensuring that all required documentation meets the necessary regulations.

Due to the sometimes superficial knowledge in the areas of production, service and even more so decommissioning, more in-depth analysis would likely reveal significantly more use cases for AI.

These additional use cases could span different stages of the product lifecycle, from improving maintenance strategies to optimising decommissioning processes, ultimately leading to more efficient and cost-effective solutions.

As AI technologies continue to evolve, further exploration of these areas may uncover opportunities for increased automation, better decision making and improved system reliability.

Despite all this, the potential of AI for these applications is shown in the graphic in fig. 5.12.

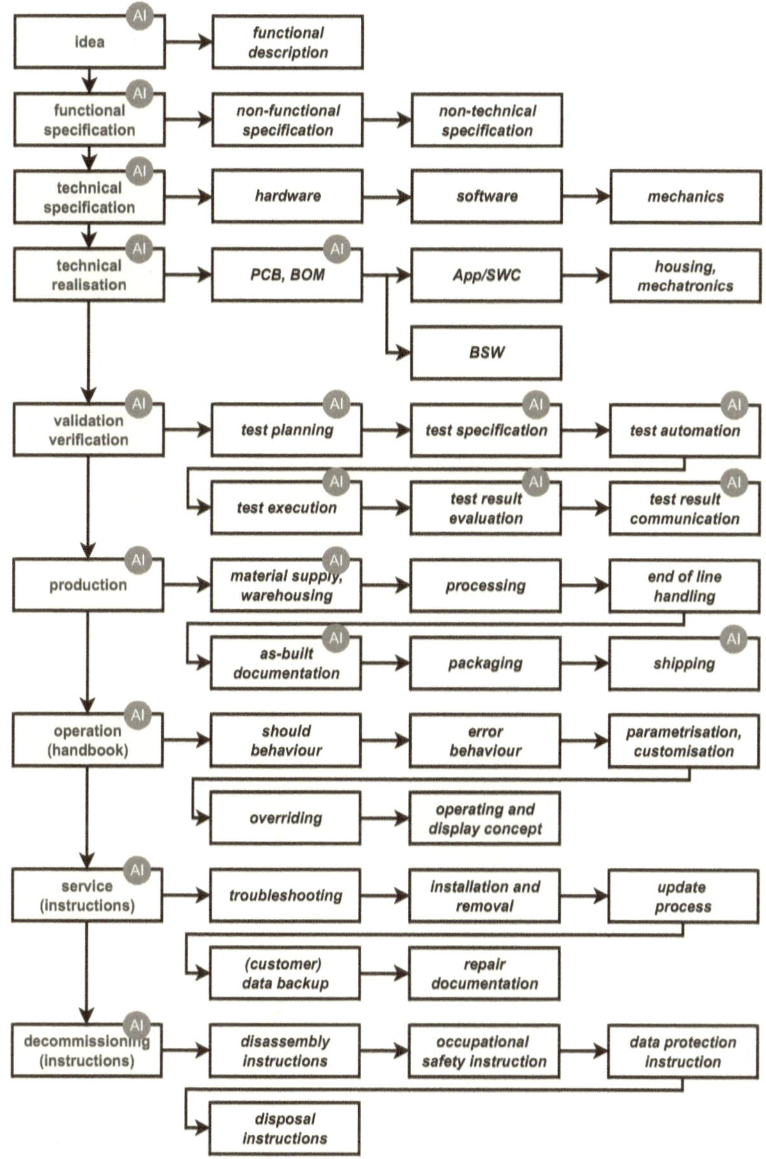

Fig. 5.12.: PLC - Potential Fields of AI Application

Part II.

Functional Safety

6. Applicability ISO 26262

First, I would like to take a look at the applicability of ISO 26262.

'This document is intended to be applied to safety-related systems that include one or more electrical and/or electronic (E/E) systems and that are *installed in series production road vehicles*, excluding mopeds.' [33, Cl. 1]

With reference to the AI applications considered as examples at page 36, this means for me that off-board applications are not the subject of ISO 26262.

'This document addresses possible hazards caused by malfunctioning behaviour of safety-related E/E systems, including interaction of these systems. It does not address hazards related to electric shock, fire, smoke, heat, radiation, toxicity, flammability, reactivity, corrosion, release of energy and similar hazards, unless directly caused by *malfunctioning behaviour* of safety-related E/E systems.' [33, Cl. 1]

The object of consideration is therefore malfunctions of E/E systems installed in series production vehicles.

Malfunctions can have various causes, e.g. design errors, software errors, hardware errors, manufacturing errors, communication errors.

It is on these issues and the related parts and clauses of ISO 26262 that I will focus my considerations.

AI-specific aspects I feel need to be highlighted are marked with a bolt.

7. EE failures of the item

If we look at the item in the generic form of the control loop, see Figure 8.3, typical E/E error patterns emerge, although no claim is made for the Figure 7.1 to be exhaustive.

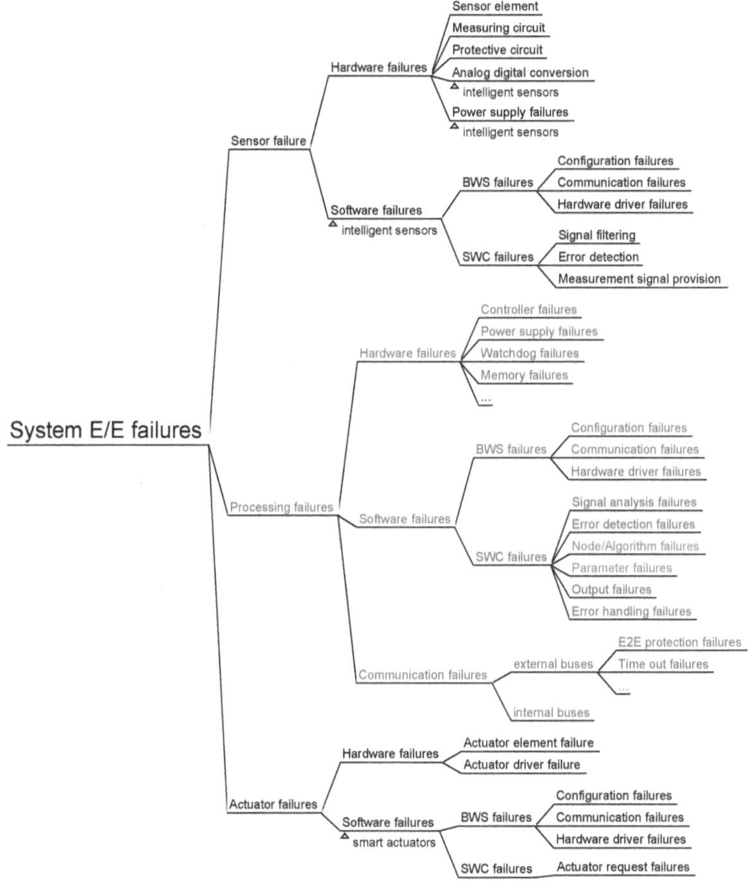

Fig. 7.1.: Generic system EE failures

As mentioned above, AI components are most likely to be found in the area of sensors and processing. Since intelligent sensors are largely similar in structure to classic Electronic Control Units (ECUs), the following analysis is based on the example of processing.

The development of the hardware [36] and software [37], marked in blue, is generally on familiar ground. The AI perimeters, marked in red, are new territory.

I have identified Parts 3 and 8 as potentially AI-specific sections of ISO 26262, which I will discuss below.

8. Concept phase

The concept phase of ISO 26262 is detailed in Part 3 [35], which deals with the development of functional safety requirements and the functional safety concept.

This phase is essential for identifying potential hazards, defining safety objectives and establishing safety measures early in the product lifecycle to ensure a robust foundation for subsequent development stages.

8.1. Clause 5 - Item definition

The basis for a development according to ISO 26262 is a sustainable Item definition [25].

"... to define and describe the item[1], its functionality, dependencies on, and interaction with, the driver, the environment and other items *at the vehicle level...*" [35, Cl. 5.1]

The item can therefore be seen as a control loop and described accordingly, as described above.

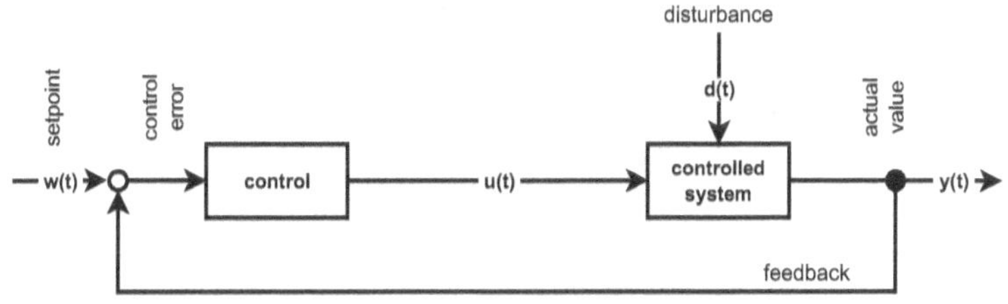

Fig. 8.1.: Control loop diagram

---

[1]   An item is a 'system or combination of systems, ... that **implements a function** or **part of a function at the vehicle level**' [33, Cl. 3.84], i.e. the customer function to be developed in its entirety.

A relatively detailed examination of the control loop as the basis of electronic systems was made at the beginning of the book.

Decomposition is a well-established method in functional safety engineering, often employed to break down complex systems into smaller, manageable components for analysis, validation, and verification.

If the controller is decomposed into its functional components, a simplified representation of the elements required for the implementation of the function is obtained.

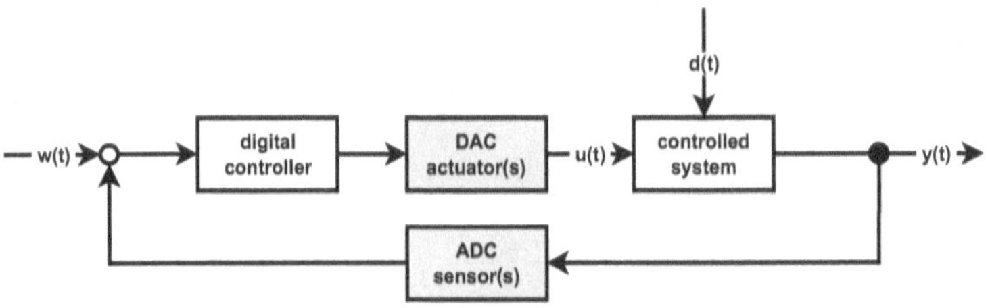

Fig. 8.2.: Item decomposition into its elements

The item definition must therefore describe the entire functionality, which also includes the elements without an AI component.

It is rather unlikely that the elements are contained just in one ECU. The (multiple) use of intelligent sensors and actuators is common. Therefore, it makes sense to supplement the communication interfaces, marked in fig. 8.3.

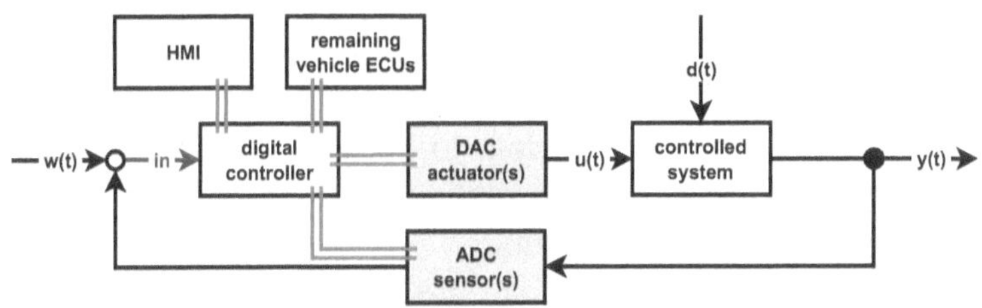

Fig. 8.3.: Elements communication for item functionality

Artificial intelligence can significantly enhance the processing capabilities within a control loop. Its applications are diverse and can be divided into two main areas: the **processing element** and the **sensors**.

For the processing element, AI algorithms can be integrated to analyse and interpret complex data patterns, optimise control strategies or predict system behaviour in real time.

This integration improves decision making and adapts the control process to dynamic conditions.

Intelligent actuators with AI support are of course also conceivable[2], but at least from a software perspective they rely on the same basic architecture as in fig. 3.11.

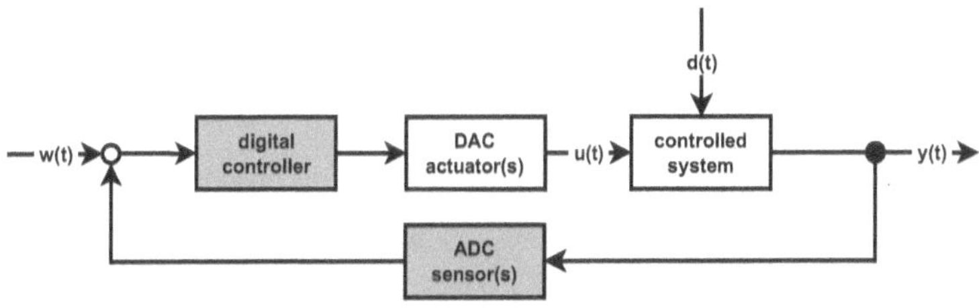

Fig. 8.4.: AI Elements for item functionality

---

[2]   e.g. intelligent priority handling of multi-channel actuator requests (multiple functions requesting the same actuator)

In addition to a clear assignment of the AI components to the object, detailled requirements for the ML need to be specified.

These include the type of data to be used, issues of scalability and efficiency, and information about the resources and infrastructure likely to be required.

In addition to clearly defined learning objectives, the expected prediction accuracy, i.e. the rate at which predictions are correct, needs to be described.

The functional view of the Item definition is thus supplemented by the AI specifics, which requires corresponding specialist knowledge.

8.2. Hazard and risk assessment

The goal of the Hazard Analysis and Risk Assessment (HARA) is 'to identify and to classify the hazardous events caused by **malfunctioning behaviour of the item**' [35, Cl. 6.1].

It follows that the malfunction behaviour of the processing, actuating and sensing elements must be considered at the vehicle level.

The 'malfunctioning behaviour' of the AI elements is the algorithm failure. This leads to a rather general consideration of the effects of algorithm failures, **ultimately resulting in erroneous predictions**.

Figure 8.5 presents possible root causes for erroneous predictions:

- falsified predictions due to incorrect input data (b)
- no or delayed predictions (c)
- falsified output of predictions (c)
- faulty algorithms
- falsified parameters
- software failures host system (e)
- hardware failures host system (f)

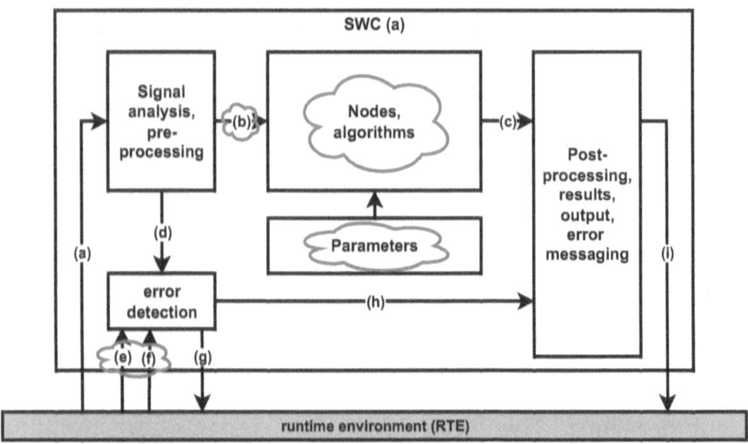

Fig. 8.5.: Potential E/E failures in AI applications

The root cause of this prediction failure is irrelevant in the context of HARA, even if the logic already suggests errors for faulty input data, the algorithms or the parameterisation.

In HARA, all operational situations are analysed for the item in which a failure would lead to a hazardous event.

8.2.1. Challange 1 - Identification E/E error based AI behaviour

A particular challenge is to analyse the prediction results of the AI for pure E/E errors and to correctly evaluate their effects with severity (S), controllability (C) and exposure (E).

NO OUTPUT DATA In this case, the AI is not producing any output due to a malfunction in the input/output processing pipeline. This could be due to signal loss, communication failure or sensor malfunction.

The challenge here is to detect the absence of data and ensure that the system can handle this scenario, either by notifying the operator or by entering a fail-safe mode.

IMPLAUSIBLE OUTPUT DATA   Implausible output data refers to predictions or results that, although numerically valid, are inconsistent with the expected behaviour of the system. For example, the AI may predict a sensor value that is physically impossible (e.g. a temperature outside an expected range).

Identifying such implausible outcomes is critical to avoiding incorrect decisions that could lead to safety hazards or inefficiencies. Methods such as anomaly detection or checking against other system variables can help to flag implausible outputs.

OUTPUT DATA OUT OF RANGE   This type of error occurs when the AI generates output data that exceeds the predefined operating limits of the system.   For example, a temperature reading above the safe threshold for the system could be flagged as an error.

The AI system must be able to detect such out-of-range values and either correct them, signal an error, or initiate predefined corrective actions such as shutting down affected subsystems to prevent further damage.

8.2.2. Challenge 2 - Assessment of safety functions

When preparing the HARA, it is important to bear in mind that the assessment can be carried out **without measures to minimise risk or correct errors**. So how to evaluate severity, controllability and exposure if the function to be developed is a safety measure?

SEVERITY   Based on the Item definition, personal injuries are to be expected in the event of failure of the item, which are then assigned a severity according to a known scheme [35, Table 1].

Since safety functions are usually developed to prevent fatal injuries, a S3 can be assumed.

CONTROLLABILITY Assessing the controllability is likely to be much more difficult. Depending on the function of the item, the expectations of the vehicle user[3] or even habituation effects[4] should be included in the controllability.

Conservatively assessed, the driver is not able to take over the function of the item himself, which therefore corresponds to a C3 [35, Table 3].

EXPOSURE This is where I see the greatest difficulty in making a proper assessment.

What is the probability of the occurrence of a random safety-critical event that the functionality of the item is intended to prevent or at least minimise the impact of? Which exposure should be chosen?

A situation catalog [9] does not help here, as only the standard driving situations are assessed, but not the random safety-critical events.

Statistically, there was one fatal road accident[5] for every 230,000 kilometres[6] driven in Germany in 2020. At an estimated average speed of 60 km/h, that would be about 3800 hours or just under 160 days of travel time. Even with these figures, one can speak of a very low probability, which corresponds to E1 [35, Table 2].

---

[3]   e.g. Emergency Braking Assist - the user's expectation that the vehicle will brake for me, I do not have to pay attention.

[4]   e.g. Emergency Braking Assist - drivers are no longer used to emergency braking

[5]   `https://de.statista.com/statistik/daten/studie/161724/umfrage/verkehrstote-in-deutschland-monatszahlen/`

[6]   `https://www.kba.de/DE/Statistik/Kraftverkehr/VerkehrKilometer/vk_inlaenderfahrleistung/2020/2020_vk_kurzbericht.html`

RESULTING ASIL   The determined values S3, C3 and E1 result in an ASIL A [35, Table 4].

However, the general gut feeling is that this value is a little too low. How can a safety function be rated so low? Usually, one sees an ASIL B for safety functions. How the respective derivation is, remains to be seen.

Safety Goals

Defining a safety goal from the situation and the hazard from HARA is comparatively simple for 'classical' functions.

It must be ensured that an error in the item does not cause a hazard in the situation in question or is reduced to an acceptable minimum.

Finding safety goals for AI based safety functions becomes problematic. What goals are possible here at all? Preventing failures is certainly one measure, but what are the acceptance criteria, such as percentage availability?

In my personal opinion, availability is a useful metric, but the extent to which it is technically feasible remains to be seen, as it must be correlated with the data quality provided to AI.

Finally, sensors[7] can also deliver insufficient or even distorted signals to the AI due to environmental factors.

Therefore, availability would have to be considered as a proportion of the time that the system is error free.

It would also make safe sense to inform the driver about the unavailability in the event of an error or insufficient sensor

---

[7]   Radar sensors can be disturbed by external influences such as electromagnetic interference, weather conditions, metallic obstacles, reflections and other radio sources.
Cameras can be affected by poor lighting, glare, dirt on the lens, physical obstructions or weather conditions.

data quality, in order to create awareness and increased attention. However, this approach is applicable at most for vehicles up to SAE level 4, i.e. driver availability is assumed.

Such an approach is no longer applicable for fully automated vehicles. Which failure rates are still permissible here would presumably have to be defined by the company or the legislator.

For further consideration, therefore, only the functional aspect of the safety goals will be considered.

9. Challenge Software development

If you look at the details, you will see that the programming, although complex, is still subject to the previous methods. At its core, AI is essentially just a parameterised algorithm, and therefore fundamentally code.

This perspective allows us to draw parallels between traditional software development and AI development, as both involve the manipulation and configuration of parameters to achieve a desired result.

This brings us back to familiar territory. After all, working with parameterisable algorithms is nothing new. From hard-coded parameters to more flexible, separately flashable parameter sets (even with Over The Air (OTA) updates), various methods of managing and updating parameters have been successfully used in various Electronic Control Units (ECUs).

These approaches have become standard practice in many embedded systems, particularly in automotive applications where the ability to modify or update parameters remotely is becoming increasingly important.

So what makes AI components complex from a programming perspective? The main drivers of complexity are the number of nodes in the neural network, the implementation of different algorithms, and the activation functions used. Each of these elements adds layers of complexity. The number of nodes and layers in an artificial neural network (ANN) can increase exponentially as the network learns more complex patterns.

Similarly, the choice of activation functions, which determine how the network processes inputs, can significantly affect both the behaviour and performance of the network. These factors, combined with the need for efficient data handling, optimisation and training processes, contribute to the inherent complexity of AI systems.

However, it is important to note that this complexity can be mitigated through the use of well-established frameworks and tools. Modern frameworks such as TensorFlow, PyTorch and Keras provide pre-built functionality that simplifies the implementation of neural networks and helps manage the complexity associated with configuring, training and deploying AI models.

These frameworks allow developers to focus on higher-level design and application logic, while abstracting much of the underlying complexity.

In the following, I will go through the clauses of Part 6 of ISO 26262 and the related work products and try to identify specific considerations for AI.

The application of the standard to AI systems requires careful attention to the unique characteristics of these technologies, such as their dynamic nature and the challenges of ensuring safety and reliability in highly complex, parameterised systems.

9.1. Clause 5 - General topics for the product development at the software level

ISO 26262-6, which focuses on the software development process for automotive safety-related systems, outlines critical activities and work products.

However, when applying this standard to AI components, particularly those based on supervised learning or neural networks, certain nuances arise that are not explicitly covered by the traditional methods of the standard.

These aspects mainly revolve around the unique nature of AI systems and the associated challenges in their development and verification.

AI system Design and Development

ISO 26262-6 emphasises the importance of software design, development and validation. However, AI components present additional challenges due to their inherent characteristics:

- AI systems are non-deterministic.
- During training, AI systems learn dynamic parameters.

In certain cases, AI components can be treated as static libraries, especially when no further learning occurs after the training phase and the AI parameters are fixed within the overall software implementation.

It is important to evaluate and distinguish between 'learned and fixed' AI systems and 'continuously learning' systems.

The design and implementation of AI systems must take into account their iterative and evolving nature. AI system specifications should define the scope, operating conditions, training data and performance metrics.

In addition, AI design must address generalisation, uncertainty handling, and real-world performance.

Verification and Validation of AI Components

Verification and validation (V&V) of AI systems also presents unique challenges.

Clause 5 states that software verification should ensure that the system behaves according to specifications, with particular attention to safety-critical features.

In the case of AI, it is critical to distinguish between typical software errors (E/E errors) and performance deficiencies inherent in the AI's learning and prediction process.

Performance deficits, such as a failure to make predictions when the input data is outside the domain of the model, should not be considered failures. Instead, they are related to the limitations of the training process or the inadequacy of the Operational Design Domain (ODD).

Standard methods for verifying AI systems must therefore include specific tests that assess the robustness of the AI to variations in input data, its ability to handle edge cases, and its overall accuracy.

In addition, the verification strategy must include both functional and non-functional aspects of AI systems.

Functional verification ensures that the AI performs the intended task[1], while non-functional verification checks for performance metrics such as latency, scalability, and resilience to data variations.

---

[1]   e.g. object recognition, decision making

Adapting traditional methods to AI systems

Although traditional methods in ISO 26262-6, such as Fault Tree Analysis (FTA) and Failure Mode and Effects Analysis (FMEA), provide a solid foundation for the verification and validation of automotive software, they need to be adapted to the unique characteristics of AI components.

For example, while FTA and FMEA are designed to identify potential failures based on known system behaviour, AI systems require a more flexible and probabilistic approach to assess their performance under uncertainty.

Therefore, the integration of AI components into safety-critical automotive systems requires an adaptation of existing processes. This includes not only new verification activities tailored to the probabilistic nature of AI systems, but also new ways of dealing with the uncertainty and non-determinism inherent in AI-based decision making.

By addressing these challenges, the principles outlined in ISO 26262-6 can be effectively applied to ensure the safety and reliability of AI-based automotive systems.

Derivation of requirements

In particular, the derivation of AI requirements requires an item definition that is as comprehensive as possible [25]. After all, this is the only source of information that can be used at all.

When describing AI requirements, classical requirements engineering methods are used, but there are important considerations that need to be taken into account due to the inherent nature of AI systems.

Below is a breakdown of how to approach this:

CLARIFYING THE SCOPE AND BOUNDARIES In traditional requirements engineering, requirements typically define the functionality and constraints of a system in a deterministic way. However, AI systems, being probabilistic and non-deterministic, introduce additional complexities.

The scope of AI systems must clearly define what the system is intended to do, its limitations and its boundaries.

This includes specifying what types of data the system will process, under what conditions, and in particular how the system will generalise beyond its training data.

DATA REQUIREMENTS In classical systems, data input requirements are usually static and well defined. For AI, data requirements must cover not only the format, sources and volume of data, but also its diversity, representativeness and quality.

Particular attention must be paid to ensuring that the training data adequately reflects real-world scenarios to avoid biased or incomplete models.

PERFORMANCE METRICS Traditional systems define performance in terms of time, resource usage, and other measurable system behaviours. AI systems, however, require performance definitions that go beyond these traditional metrics.

Performance should include accuracy, precision, recall, F1-score (F1), robustness to unexpected inputs, and the ability of the model to generalise. In addition, AI systems need to be evaluated under uncertainty, edge cases and failure scenarios.

VALIDATION AND VERIFICATION Classical systems have well-understood validation and verification processes that ensure the system meets its requirements and performs as expected. However, AI systems present unique challenges for verification and validation due to their non-deterministic nature.

Instead of hard-coded validation criteria, AI systems must include provisions for ongoing validation through testing with both known and unknown data sets, real-time performance monitoring, and addressing performance degradation over time.

Test cases must cover various edge cases and real-world scenarios that the AI system may encounter.

ADAPTABILITY AND CONTINUOUS LEARNING Classical systems generally have fixed behaviors once deployed, but AI systems may continue learning post-deployment or remain static after training.

If the AI system is designed for continuous learning, the requirements must define how this process will be controlled and monitored to avoid new risks, such as concept drift.

SAFETY AND SECURITY Traditional safety and security requirements focus on preventing failures or malicious exploitation. For AI, additional safety considerations are necessary due to the potential unpredictability of AI systems.

These include ensuring AI components can handle adversarial inputs, ensuring robust operation in all conditions, and managing risks arising from unintended behaviors, such as AI hallucinations or decision biases.

EXPLAINABILITY AND TRANSPARENCY Traditional systems are usually designed to have predictable behaviors with understandable internal workings.

In contrast, AI systems, particularly those using complex models like deep neural networks, often operate as 'black boxes', making it difficult to understand how decisions are made.

Therefore, explainability and interpretability are critical, especially in safety-critical applications, such as automotive systems, where decisions made by AI must be transparent and justifiable.

KEY CONSIDERATIONS WHEN APPLYING CLASSICAL REQUIREMENTS ENGINEERING TO AI Unlike traditional systems, AI systems are probabilistic and not fully predictable.

Therefore, the classical requirements engineering approach, which often assumes deterministic behaviour, needs to be adapted to account for this inherent uncertainty in AI.

Requirements for AI systems should explicitly address how this uncertainty will be managed, such as defining acceptable performance thresholds, confidence levels for predictions, and error rates.

AI systems also evolve and improve over time through continuous learning and model refinement. Unlike traditional systems, which are typically static once implemented, AI systems are dynamic.

As such, classical requirements, which typically assume fixed specifications, must remain flexible to accommodate ongoing updates, retraining and refinement.

This includes defining how model versions are managed, how updates are validated, and how compatibility with existing systems is ensured.

In addition, the ability of AI systems to generalise and perform well under varying conditions must be part of the requirements.

Traditional requirements engineering often involves exhaustive testing under known conditions, which is not feasible for AI systems due to their dependence on large, diverse data sets. Therefore, AI-specific requirements should address how the system will handle unseen data, outliers, and dynamic environments.

This includes defining performance metrics that measure the robustness and generalisation capabilities of the system, and outlining strategies for evaluating the model on diverse datasets to ensure reliable performance in real-world, unpredictable scenarios.

CONCLUSION AI requirements can indeed be described using classical requirements engineering methods, but the unique characteristics of AI—such as their probabilistic nature, reliance on data, continuous learning, and the need for explainability—demand special attention.

Requirements must be flexible, comprehensive, and include ongoing evaluations of AI behavior in real-world conditions.

The result is AI-specific software requirements.

Implementation of AI requirements in AI libraries

AI requirements are implemented in dedicated AI libraries such as TensorFlow[2], PyTorch[3] or Keras[4].

Implementing the libraries requires a high level of AI expertise. However, AutoML frameworks and toolkits such as NVIDIA DRIVE Constellation, H2O.ai Driverless AI, IBM Watson AutoAI or DataRobot can provide support.

In the context of ISO 26262-6 Clause 5, several additional considerations are required to ensure compliance with safety-critical standards:

---

[2]   Google Brain, C++ open source software library, 2015
[3]   Meta AI, Python open source library, 2016
[4]   François Chollet, open source library, 2015

TOOL QUALIFICATION   All libraries and toolkits must undergo a qualification process to ensure their suitability for safety-critical applications. This includes evaluation of their reliability, fault behaviour and compatibility with ASIL requirements.

While this qualification process is standard practice for conventional software tools, its direct application to AI components is limited.

AI inherently produces probabilistic and non-deterministic results that challenge traditional qualification methods. As a result, the surrounding toolchain - including data pre-processing, model training pipelines and validation environments - plays a much more critical role in ensuring compliance and reliability.

DETERMINISTIC BEHAVIOUR   The AI implementation must minimise stochastic or non-deterministic behaviour to meet the requirement for predictable and reliable execution in safety-critical systems.

It is important to distinguish between the 'error-freeness' of the system implementation and the 'prediction accuracy' of the AI model.

While faultlessness refers to the correct and deterministic functioning of the software components, prediction accuracy refers to the statistical performance of the AI model in fulfilling its task.

Both aspects require independent consideration: the software must be deterministic and free of implementation errors, even though the predictions of the AI model are inherently uncertain due to the probabilistic nature of machine learning.

TRACEABILITY The AI requirements must be fully traceable from definition through design, implementation and verification. This includes documenting how the library[5] supports each requirement.

The AI framework makes it difficult to map requirements directly to AI components.

If there are no (automatable) interfaces between the AI framework and the requirements database, there must be process assurance of how the implementation of the requirements is integrated into the AI toolchain.

Given the complexity and inherent uncertainties of AI systems, achieving precise traceability may not always be straightforward. However, it is essential to describe as accurately as possible the mapping between requirements and the corresponding steps in the AI toolchain, including data preparation, model training, evaluation and deployment.

This documentation ensures a clear understanding of how safety-critical requirements are addressed throughout the AI development lifecycle.

CODE ANALYSIS AND TESTING Comprehensive static and dynamic code analysis must be performed on the libraries to identify and mitigate potential risks. This includes the use of automated tools and manual code reviews.

However, applying these methods to AI components raises specific challenges:

---

[5]   included in AI development framework

- **Feasibility and Scope**: *Static code analysis* can be applied to the framework and implementation code[6], but its utility for analyzing the inner workings of AI models, such as neural networks, is limited.
  Dynamic code analysis may provide insights into runtime behavior but often cannot fully capture the non-deterministic nature of AI components.
- **Specific Considerations for AI Components**: For AI systems, code analysis should focus on areas such as:
  - Data preprocessing pipelines, ensuring robustness against incorrect or adversarial inputs.
  - Model inference code, verifying that it handles edge cases and unexpected input gracefully.
  - Resource management in the runtime environment, such as GPU utilization and memory handling.
- **Limitations of Traditional Methods**: Traditional static and dynamic analysis tools may not address issues specific to AI, such as biases in training data, convergence issues in model training, or sensitivity to input variations.
- **Augmenting with Specialised Techniques**: In addition to traditional methods, techniques such as model explainability tools, adversarial robustness testing, and validation of probabilistic outputs should be incorporated to address AI-specific risks.

While traditional code analysis provides a solid foundation for ensuring the reliability of the supporting software, specialized approaches are needed to evaluate and mitigate risks specific to AI components effectively.

ERROR HANDLING AND SAFETY MECHANISMS   The AI libraries shall include robust error handling mechanisms to detect, isolate and mitigate software errors.

---

[6]   e.g., Python scripts, C++ libraries

These mechanisms shall be consistent with the overall security goals of the system. In particular, AI frameworks often provide built-in error detection and safety mechanisms, such as invalid input handling, exception management, and failure recovery strategies.

Where available, these features should be fully exploited to ensure that the AI system can respond to runtime problems without compromising security. The associated processes should be reviewed and adapted if necessary.

In addition, AI-specific security mechanisms, such as protection against adversarial attacks, data poisoning, or model inversion, should be considered and integrated into the overall error handling approach.

The use of these mechanisms should be systematically verified to ensure that they meet the requirements for safety-critical systems.

RESOURCE MANAGEMENT The implementation must ensure efficient and secure use of memory and computing resources, avoiding problems such as memory leaks or buffer overflows.

In AI systems, particular attention must be paid to the unique resource management challenges that arise from the computational demands of machine learning models. These include the handling of large datasets, model parameters, and the computational load during training and inference.

In particular, AI systems often use specialised hardware such as multi-core CPUs, Graphics Processing Units (GPUs), neural network cores[7] and field-programmable gate arrays (FP-GAs) to optimise performance.

---

[7] e.g. tensor cores

It is essential to ensure that these resources are used effectively and that resource allocation is handled efficiently to avoid bottlenecks or hardware-specific problems such as memory contention in multi-core systems or improper resource partitioning across heterogeneous hardware components.

Proper memory management and synchronisation between these components should be explicitly addressed, particularly when using hardware accelerators such as GPUs or FPGAs, to ensure that the system operates predictably and within its resource limits.

DOCUMENTATION Libraries need to be accompanied by detailed documentation about their architecture, interfaces, limitations and security considerations.

In AI systems, much of the underlying functionality and implementation details are often abstracted or 'hidden' within the AI frameworks, making comprehensive documentation more challenging.

It is important to assess whether the framework can automatically generate documentation on critical components such as the model architecture, training pipelines, and specific configurations used during the development process.

This (automated) documentation output should be integrated and process-embedded into the development lifecycle to ensure that all relevant details are captured without relying on manual documentation, which may be incomplete or error-prone.

In addition, in line with cybersecurity requirements [31], the output of a Software Bill of Material (SBOM) is required. An SBOM provides a comprehensive list of the components used in the system, including any third-party libraries or dependencies, and is essential for tracking potential vulnerabilities and ensuring compliance with cybersecurity standards.

Ensuring that the AI toolchain is capable of generating an SBOM and incorporating it into the security documentation is an essential part of the process.

Definition of hyperparameters

The definition of hyperparameters plays a crucial role in balancing both accuracy and predictability in AI models, especially for safety-critical applications. Limiting the value ranges of hyperparameters can help reduce model instability, but it may also decrease accuracy.

For instance, a lower learning rate may improve stability but hinder efficient learning.

Larger batch sizes can enhance accuracy but may introduce instability, whereas smaller batch sizes tend to improve stability, potentially at the cost of accuracy. Deeper models capture more complex patterns, boosting accuracy, but they may reduce predictability due to increased risks of overfitting and instability.

Higher dropout rates improve generalization and accuracy but make the model more volatile, which reduces predictability. In safety-critical systems, it is essential to maintain a balance between accuracy and predictability, ensuring that the system remains reliable and deterministic.

Hyperparameters should be chosen carefully to guarantee stability and error-free behavior under various operational conditions. The value ranges of hyperparameters must be limited to minimize the risk of non-deterministic behavior while optimizing performance.

A comprehensive evaluation of hyperparameters' effects on both accuracy and safety is neccessary to ensuring compliance with safety standards, such as ISO 26262.

Additionally, proper documentation of hyperparameter settings and their impact on model behavior is essential for traceability and safety analysis.

As with the implementation in the AI libraries, the definition of the hyperparameters as a starting point for learning requires a high level of expertise on the part of the developer.

However, the hyperparameters can be optimised using various tools such as Optuna, SigOpt or Hyperopt.

AI Training

The next step in developing an AI application is training. Various tools and frameworks can be used, such as TensorFlow, PyTorch, Keras, Caffe or MATLAB.

In addition to the training tool, tools are needed to provide quality training data. Of course, these data collection tools are highly dependent on the specific application. For supervised learning applications, labelling or tagging functions are also required.

Due to the potentially large amount of data, databases should also be considered as a tool.

However, in the context of safety-critical applications, specific aspects must be considered during the AI training process, in accordance with ISO 26262-6 Clause 5:

- **Qualification of Training Tools**: The tools used for AI training[8] must be qualified to ensure they are suitable for safety-critical applications.

---

[8] e.g., TensorFlow, PyTorch

- **Verification of Training Data**: The quality of the training data must be verified to ensure it is correct, complete, and free of errors. Inaccurate or incomplete data can negatively affect the model and introduce safety risks.
- **Model Performance Verification**: The trained model must be validated to ensure it meets the defined safety requirements and performs correctly under various conditions, including fault tolerance for erroneous input data.
- **Traceability of the Training Process**: The entire training process[9], including data, parameters, and model selection, must be traceable to ensure that the safety requirements of the system are met.
- **Error Handling during Training**: The model must be trained to handle anomalies or erroneous data appropriately to ensure model stability and safety.

Verification

The final step is to test the trained AI for functionality and prediction accuracy.

This process step differs from the learning process only in that no iterative adjustments are made to the AI parameters and only the prediction accuracy is checked.

It is important that the test data used in this step meet certain quality requirements. They should represent the intended application scenarios comprehensively and without bias. In addition, the test data must remain separate from the training data to prevent any form of data leakage and to ensure an unbiased evaluation of the model. Importantly, test data must never be used for further training or fine-tuning of the AI.

In line with ISO 26262-6, the following additional aspects must be considered during verification:

---

[9]   graphical representations strongly recommended

- **Conformance to ASIL requirements**: All verification activities must comply with the application's safety critical level (ASIL). Higher ASIL levels require more stringent validation and testing.
- **Fault Tolerance and Safety Objectives**: The system must be tested for compliance with defined safety goals, including scenarios involving hardware or software failures.
- **Traceability**: All test cases and results shall be fully traceable to the original safety requirements to ensure consistency and completeness.
- **Tool qualification**: Tools used for testing and verification shall be qualified according to their impact on the safety lifecycle.
- **Robustness and Edge Cases**: The AI system shall demonstrate reliable operation in edge cases and failure scenarios, ensuring robustness and predictable behaviour.

Testing must include performance evaluations under various operational constraints to ensure safety and compliance under real-world conditions. All verification and validation activities should be thoroughly documented to meet regulatory and safety standards.

Integration

There are several ways to integrate the parameterised AI algorithms into the Software Components, depending on the development strategy and the development partners involved.

In the simplest case, the algorithms are integrated as source code into the code of the Software Components. However, integration as compiled binaries is also possible. The latter would be an option if the AI shares are provided or purchased by development partners.

The integration itself is done through the host system's development environment, which can be either model-based or high-level language. The evaluation of this tool chain is similar to that of existing development environments.

This, as well as all the downstream steps in the software development process, follow established software development processes.

WP: Documentation of the software development environment

The requirements of Clause 5 'Product development at the software level' result in this work product [37, 5.5.1].

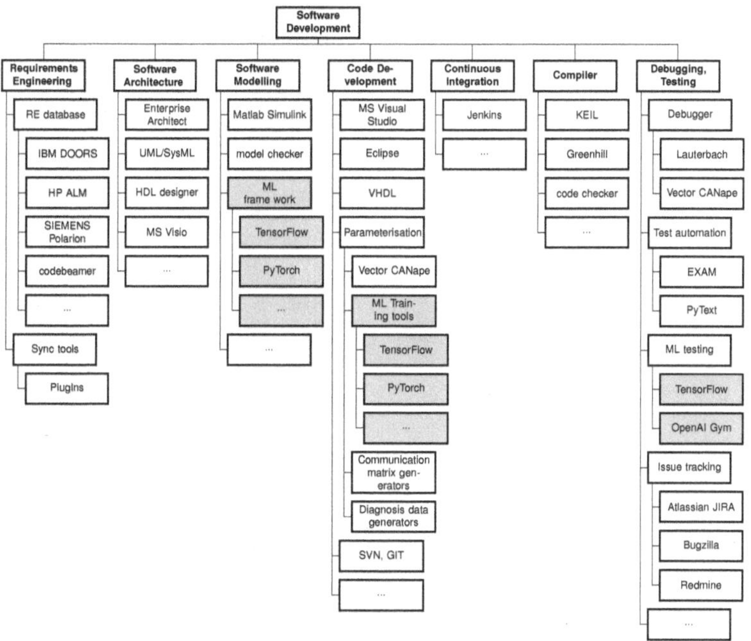

Fig. 9.1.: Generic software development tool chain

Among other things, the processes, tools, programming languages and guidelines used are to be presented in terms of usability, compatibility and consistency in the overall context of hardware and software development.

The AI-specific tools should therefore be included in the existing documentation of the software development environment and analysed according to the above-mentioned aspects.

- AI framework and libraries
- training tools or frameworks
- verification tools

It should be noted that these tools are often not automotive-specific developments and compliance with ISO 26262 cannot be expected.

9.2. Clause 6 - Specification of software safety requirements

The development of software safety requirements for AI-based functions is no different from that for classical functions. Therefore, no specific considerations are required.

WP: Software safety requirements specification

This work product [37, 6.5.1] considers the safety requirements in the safe execution of the basic function, safe or degraded states, monitoring functions, self-tests, on-board and off-board diagnostics, aspects of production, maintenance and decommissioning.

This work product considers safety requirements in the safe execution of the basic function, safe or degraded states, monitoring functions, self-tests, on-board and off-board diagnostics, production, maintenance and decommissioning aspects.

Issues such as freedom from interference (FFI) and software fault tolerance capabilities are also analysed.

Most AI-specific topics relating to requirements have already been described in section 'Derivation of requirements' on p. 105.

WP: Hardware-software interface (HSI) specification (refined)

The specification of the hardware-software interface (HSI) in the context of AI needs to address several key considerations:

SPECIALISED HARDWARE   AI models, especially deep learning algorithms, often require specialised hardware[10].

The HSI specification should define how such hardware supports AI software without compromising system security.

ERROR HANDLING   AI systems require specific error handling mechanisms at the hardware level, especially for hardware failures[11].

The HSI shall describe how these are detected and mitigated.

SYNCHRONISATION   AI systems require close synchronisation between hardware and software.

The HSI should ensure that delays or latencies in the processing of AI models are taken into account.

REAL TIME AND RELIABILITY   AI models require real-time processing for safety-critical systems.

The HSI should define how the system ensures both real-time operation and reliable results.

DATA INTEGRITY   The integrity of data exchanged between AI hardware and software shall be ensured to avoid data corruption or loss.

RESOURCE MANAGEMENT   AI algorithms often require parallel processing and large computing resources.

The HSI should specify how the hardware handles these requirements efficiently.

---

[10]   e.g. GPUs, Tensor Processing Units (TPUs), FPGAs
[11]   e.g. memory errors

WP: Software verification report

For AI systems in safety-critical applications, this work product [37, 6.5.3] needs to address the following AI-specific issues:

VERIFICATION OF MODEL BEHAVIOUR Verification should focus on how the AI model behaves with respect to its safety requirements, including edge cases and failure modes[12].

UNCERTAINTY AND CONFIDENCE LEVELS The report shall describe how uncertainty in AI predictions is handled, including confidence levels and safe operational behaviour despite uncertain outputs.

REQUIREMENTS TRACEABILITY AI-specific requirements[13] should be traceable from safety objectives to model behaviour and testing to ensure full compliance with safety standards.

This is particularly true for tool breaks, i.e. the transitions from requirements engineering tools to AI frameworks and back to the test specification.

EXPLAINABILITY AND INTERPRETABILITY The report should include how AI decisions are made interpretable, ensuring transparency and traceability of the model's actions.

FAILURE MODES AND ERROR HANDLING AI failures[14] should be assessed, with clear mitigation strategies for error handling.

---

[12]   e.g., adversarial input or out-of-distribution data

[13]   accuracy, robustness

[14]   e.g. incorrect predictions or adversarial attacks

PERFORMANCE UNDER VARYING CONDITIONS Verification must include testing under different operational conditions, especially with new or unseen data, to ensure robustness and security.

9.3. Clause 7 - Software architectural design

Firstly, a clarification of the subject of software architectural design.

Software architectural design encompasses the entire ECU software, see also Figure 3.11.

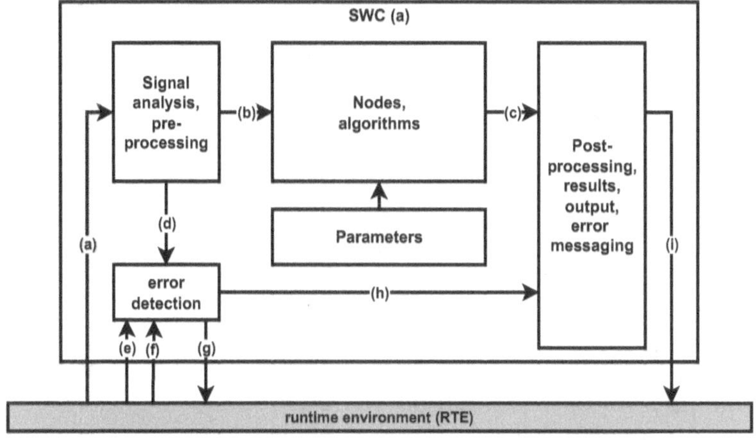

Fig. 9.2.: Software architectural design

However, only the components with an AI specifics should be examined in detail, i.e. the nodes and algorithms.

Since the node cluster is a comparatively simple interconnection of the nodes, see Figure 2.12, the main focus is on the programming of the nodes themselves.

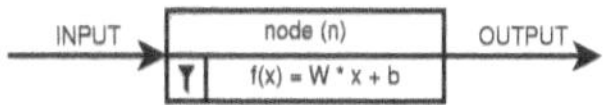

Fig. 9.3.: Single node, see also Figure 2.11

In the following, the workproducts of clause 7 are applied to the single node.

WP: Software architectural design specification

The architectural integration of AI was already visible in Figure 9.2. Depending on the level of detail of the software architectural design specification the AI component is a control function like in traditional ECUs. Therefore, this work product [37, 7.5.1] **does not contain any AI specifics**.

However, in terms of self-diagnosis, the basic function of the AI application should be ensured in the architectural considerations by means of startup tests with positive and negative samples[15].

WP: Safety analysis report

In this work product [37, 7.5.2], the analysis methods for verifying the software architecture are selected and their results are provided.

Since the AI behaves like a traditional function from an error perspective, **no AI specifics** are required.

WP: Dependent failures analysis report

The aim of the Dependent failure analysis (DFA) [37, 7.5.3] is to show that the elements of the software architecture do not influence each other. When the AI component is considered as a function, special procedures are also expected.

Since AI components not only place a particular load on the processor, but should ideally run on dedicated hardware, cross-interference can be minimised through clever processor selection and core allocation.

---

[15]   see also Signal analysis, Pre-processing at page 56

WP: Software verification report

The purpose of this work product [37, 7.5.4] is to ensure that the verification of the software architecture has been correctly planned [38, 9.5.1], designed [38, 9.5.2] and successfully executed [38, 9.5.3].

While the planning and execution of architecture testing does not involve any AI-specific features, the design of test cases requires a deeper look.

The following methods for the verification of the **software architectural design** [37, Tab.4] are commonly used to verify the software architecture of AI systems:

- **1a Inspection of the design**, difficult to performe because complex programming must be analysed in addition to in-depth mathematical knowledge
- **1b Inspection of the design**, checks the quality of the programming along the mathematics of the algorithms
- **1c Simulation of the dynamic behaviour of the design**, only useful for load determination
- **1d Prototype generation**, scaled-down model? 8-bit instead of 32-bit?
- **1e Formal verification**, which uses formal models and logical proof methods to mathematically prove that certain properties of the software architecture are fulfilled
- **1f Control flow analysis**, verifies programming quality and avoids dead code
- **1g Data flow analysis**, not useful at node level, as input data always arrives pre-filtered
- **1h Scheduling analysis**, verifies execution time depending on the use case and cycle time of the data provided at node level, upscaling may be incorrect

Distinguishing between E/E failures and performance degradation is likely to be particularly challenging, especially in the context of AI applications where the boundaries between these two categories are not always clearly defined.

E/E failures typically result from deterministic failures in hardware or software components, such as broken connections, memory corruption, or computational errors. These failures can be systematically identified and addressed using established fault detection and diagnostic techniques.

In contrast, performance failures occur when an AI system fails to deliver the expected functional results, often due to limitations in the training data, insufficient generalisation capabilities, or unforeseen edge cases in the operational environment.

Such failures are inherently more complex to diagnose because they do not arise from discrete, identifiable faults in the system, but rather from a mismatch between the system's capabilities and the requirements of the application.

Despite this complexity, from a formal point of view **no AI specifics** are expected in the work product related to the differentiation of these problems. The processes and documentation required to evaluate E/E failures and performance deficits are aligned with existing standards and practices, such as those outlined in ISO 26262 and ISO 21448.

These standards already provide a framework for assessing and systematically addressing safety risks, regardless of whether the underlying functionality involves traditional software or AI components.

Ultimately, while the challenge lies in the nuanced analysis required to separate these categories, the basic methodologies and expectations for their treatment remain consistent with established engineering practices.

9.4. Clause 8 - Software unit design and implementation

WP: Software unit design specification

The software unit design specification [37, 8.5.1] could contain a large AI-specific component if the individual nodes within the neural network were programmed manually. This would introduce significant complexity, as each node would require a bespoke implementation of activation functions, algorithms and connections to other nodes.

In practice, however, the programming of activation functions, algorithms and their aggregation into the appropriate nodes is tool-based. These tools automate much of the process, using predefined libraries and frameworks to construct and parameterise the neural network architecture.

This tool-based approach reduces the design effort, as shown in Figure 3.11, to signal analysis, error detection, result output and error handling, which are tasks very similar to those found in non-AI applications.

For example, the design of input signal processing pipelines and output validation layers can be standardised across both AI and non-AI systems, simplifying integration into the broader software development workflow.

This standardisation also ensures that the resulting design specification conforms to established automotive safety standards, such as ISO 26262, without requiring significant deviations for AI-specific features.

It is worth noting that while the underlying AI model may introduce complexity in the training and validation phases, this is not directly reflected in the design specification of the software unit. Instead, the focus remains on defining the interfaces, dependencies and error handling mechanisms required for reliable operation within the host system.

WP: Software unit implementation

The software unit implementation [37, 8.5.2] represents the translation of the design specification into executable code, whether through graphical programming environments or traditional programming languages.

This work product includes the instantiation of the neural network architecture, activation functions and associated algorithms.

If the activation functions and algorithms are developed using tool-based approaches, such as frameworks like TensorFlow, PyTorch or MATLAB, there are again no significant **AI-specific features** to consider at this stage. In this case, the **AI content is a black box** and is treated in the same way as libraries or provided object files.

These frameworks provide optimised, pre-validated implementations of common components, reducing the need for custom programming and ensuring compatibility with automotive-grade hardware and software platforms.

The primary focus during this phase is to ensure that the generated code integrates seamlessly into the target environment. This includes meeting performance constraints, such as real-time processing requirements, and safety-critical standards, such as memory management and error detection.

In addition, the use of standardised test tools and methodologies at this stage ensures that the implementation meets the safety and functional requirements outlined in the specification.

This approach minimises deviations between design and implementation, while maintaining consistency with the overall system architecture.

9.5. Clause 9 - Software unit verification

WP: Software verification specification

The aim of this work product [37, 9.5.1] is to provide a recognisable and structured test strategy[16] as well as an appropriate test specification for all software units.

This specification serves as a blueprint for verifying that each unit meets its functional, performance, and safety requirements.

I am a strong advocate of a **holistic approach to verification**, where the development of verification strategies is treated as an integrated concept rather than isolated efforts.

A small contribution from the field: Following the principles outlined by ISTQB, this approach ensures that verification activities are comprehensive, consistent, and aligned with industry best practices.

By incorporating relevant standards such as ISO 26262, ISO 21448, and potentially ISO 21434, alongside ASPICE SUB.2[17], the verification strategy can address the full spectrum of safety, performance, and cybersecurity concerns.

This multi-standard framework allows for a balanced and thorough evaluation of the system, ensuring all critical aspects are covered while maintaining alignment with regulatory and industry expectations.

At the same time, this approach allows for verification to be considered within both the functional and systemic context.

By integrating the verification strategy across multiple standards and domains, it becomes possible to assess how in-

---

[16]   including test methodology, environment, and execution
[17]   even if no longer required in ASPICE version 4.0

dividual components and functions interact within the overall system.

This ensures that both isolated functional correctness and broader system-wide behaviours, such as performance, safety, and security, are thoroughly validated in a unified manner, offering a comprehensive understanding of the system's reliability and robustness in real-world conditions.

For this thematic excursion, I apologise.

For AI components, the specification must include considerations for both traditional software verification and **AI-specific performance evaluation**.

Traditional verification focuses on ensuring that deterministic functions operate correctly within defined parameters, such as boundary conditions, error handling, and interface behaviours.

In contrast, AI verification requires additional test cases to evaluate prediction accuracy, robustness against noise, and behaviour under edge cases or unknown inputs.

A clear and consistent separation between **E/E failures** and **AI performance deficiencies** must be ensured to align with the different safety frameworks outlined in ISO 26262 and ISO 21448.

This distinction allows for tailored test strategies: deterministic test methods for hardware/software faults and performance-oriented methodologies for AI, such as cross-validation or golden sample datasets.

A practical method of distinguishing is to use corresponding labels in the test cases.

Furthermore, the test specification should address how *real-time constraints* are tested for *onboard* AI applications. The latency and computational resource requirements of AI algorithms must be evaluated to ensure they do not interfere with other safety-critical processes.

The overlap of standards must not result in a conflict of responsibilities, advocating for the **equal treatment** of all test cases with appropriate labelling, while reserving **special handling** exclusively for safety- and SOTIF-relevant test cases.

WP: Software verification report (refined)

This work product [37, 9.5.2] represents a comprehensive documentation of the verification activities performed during the software development lifecycle.

It is refined to include detailed information about the software unit verification, making it an essential input for subsequent safety assessments.

The report includes the test methods applied, detailed descriptions of the test cases executed, and an analysis of the test results. For AI components, this means integrating **AI performance verification results** into the overall verification report.

This could include metrics such as prediction accuracy, false positive and false negative rates, and robustness testing outcomes.

AI-specific verification results should highlight how the system performs under expected operating conditions and stress scenarios. Additionally, the report must address how the system manages edge cases and unknown inputs to ensure that performance limitations are well understood and mitigated.

For example, the verification results should confirm whether the AI system behaves predictably when presented with data outside its training domain, emphasizing safe fallback mechanisms.

The integration of these results into the verification report ensures that stakeholders, including auditors and end-users, have a complete understanding of both the deterministic and performance aspects of the software.

This holistic approach ensures transparency and provides a robust foundation for evaluating the overall safety and reliability of the AI application within the host system.

The software verification report according to ISO 26262 should be created and maintained in conjunction with the results of the SOTIF evaluation of known and unknown scenarios [41, 10.8, 11.3].

It is not sufficient to consider either traditional software verification or AI performance evaluation in isolation. It is essential to combine both into a comprehensive verification approach.

This integrated view ensures that all relevant performance characteristics of the system are validated, including its robustness to unknown inputs and edge cases, which are critical for AI-based applications.

As a result, the report provides a complete and balanced picture of the system's behaviour, addressing both deterministic software faults and potential performance failures, ultimately supporting a more holistic safety assessment. Again, appropriate labelling facilitates distinction.

9.6. Clause 10 - Software integration and verification

With this process step, all software components belonging to the ECU software are combined and converted into executable code.

WP: Software verification specification (refined)

The aim of this work product [37, 10.5.1] is to demonstrate that the verification of software integration has been carried out taking into consideration:

- appropriate use of test methods
- completeness of the test cases
- consideration of the correct DUT
- appropriate test facilities

When AI models are part of the system, the following additional AI-specific aspects must be considered in the software verification process:

- **Data Validation and Quality:** Ensure that training and test data are accurate, representative, and sufficient for model performance.
- **Model Verification:** Validate the model using techniques such as cross-validation, ensuring it performs well with real-world and unseen data.
- **Explainability and Transparency:** The model's decisions must be interpretable, especially for safety-critical applications.
- **Prediction Accuracy:** Verify that the model's prediction accuracy meets predefined requirements.
- **Robustness and Fault Tolerance:** Test the model's robustness to erroneous or unexpected inputs, ensuring safe failure modes.

- **Safety Considerations, Complience:** Ensure the model complies with safety standards such as ISO 26262 and ISO 21448, and handle performance deficiencies appropriately.
- **Error Management and Feedback Loops:** If the model adapts over time, establish clear processes for error handling and continuous learning.

WP: Embedded software

This work product [37, 10.5.2] comprises the actual compilation process. Since a programming implementation of the AI components is already available from the previous process steps, no special effort is expected here.   subsection*WP: Software verification report (refined)

This work product represents the result of software integration, i.e. the machine-executable software consisting of the Software Component (SWC) and, depending on the operating system, the Basis Software (BSW).

AI specific here, as already described several times, is the concentration in testing on E/E failures.

9.7. Clause 11 - Testing of the embedded software

WP: Software verification specification (refined)

As a final step in the software verification process, this embedded software work product [37, 11.5.1] checks that the methods used are correct, that the test cases executed are described and referenced, and that they have been successfully executed.

As the focus here is also on finding E/E failures, no AI specifics are expected.

WP: Software verification report (refined)

This work product [37, 11.5.2] provides the verification result report and demonstrates that the embedded software has been tested in an appropriate test environment using appropriate methods.

It also verifies that the test cases were derived using appropriate methods and that the embedded software achieved the expected targets. Finally, the coverage of the software security requirements by the test cases is verified.

Considering pure E/E errors, there are no new AI-specific requirements for this work product.

9.8. Clause Annex C - Software configuration

AI is particularly a configured software.

WP: Configuration data specification

Configuration data are static, pre-configured parameters[18] for algorithm within a Software Component or sub-functions of the Software Component. They are therefore part of the runnables and are accordingly compiled together with the algorithm.

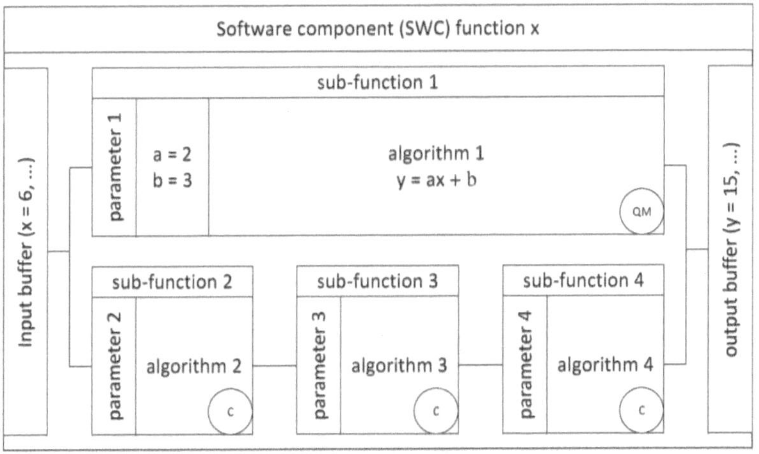

Fig. 9.4.: Configuration data explaination

This means that the node cluster parameter sets from Figure 2.13 fall into this category.

The configuration data specification [37, C.5.1] requires the provision of several pieces of information:

• purpose and use of the configuration data (explaination)

---

[18] e.g. non-vehicle specific parameters, parameters for ML algorithm

- data or data set information (data type, data size, value range, scaling, units of the configuration data)
- dependencies between configuration data
- corresponding/assigned ASIL

In the case of node cluster parameters, this background information is difficult or impossible to provide due to the training.
⚡ This is therefore specific to AI.

WP: Configuration data

The handling of configuration data within the software architecture, the software unit and the ECU as a whole is known terrain, which is why this work product [37, C.5.3] is not AI specific.

Calibration data specification, calibration data

The parameterisation of AI components is static and not vehicle-specific. Therefore, these work products [37, C.5.2, C.5.4] are not considered AI specific.

WP: Verification specification (refined)

The aim of this refinement [37, C.5.5] is the verification of the configuration and calibration data as well as their specifications, the applicability in the safety life cycle and suitable calibration processes.

Only the configuration data specification has turned out to be AI specific. All other aspects remain AI free.

WP: Verification report (refined)

This work product [37, C.5.6] ensures that the specified verification has been carried out methodically and technically correctly and that the target parameters have been met.

Taking into account, as before, the differentiation between E/E errors and performance errors, this work product is also AI free.

WP: Software architectural design specification (refined)

The aim of this work product [37, C.5.7] - apart from the misleading title - is to ensure that no unintended changes in calibration data can occur.

AI parameters are - as already described - static and therefore do not fall under calibration data. Therefore, this work product is AI free.

WP: Documentation of the software development environment (refined)

The documentation of the software development environment [37, 5.5.1] on page 119 has already been described in clause 5. This work product [37, C.5.8] deals with refinement in the event of changes to the software development environment.

As the AI frameworks are also part of the software development environment, this work product is AI specific. Methodologically, however, there are no AI specifics.

Summary AI impact software development

In principle, the software development of AI-based in-vehicle applications is little different from that of conventional software applications.

The impact of AI specifics in ISO 26262 work products is mainly limited to the extension of the development process by the machine learning part, the associated tools and additional verification steps.

Software architecture requires a close look at self-diagnosis capabilities in both conventional and AI applications. In terms of applications, AI should in particular ensure the functioning of prediction with golden samples in the sense of positive and negative sample patterns.

10. Supporting Processes

Part 8 of ISO 26262, the supporting processes, should also be checked for impact by AI specifics. Some of the work products listed here may contain AI artefacts.

The clauses 5-10, 13-16 and Annexes A und B are not specific to AI and are therefore excluded from this analysis.

10.1. Clause 11 - Confidence in the use of software tools

To identify the software tools to be evaluated, it is useful to look at the tool chain used, see Figure 9.1.

As shown in the figure, AI-specific tools are required for software **modelling**, **coding** and **testing**.

WP: Software tool criteria evaluation report

The purpose of this work product is to gain confidence in the use of software tools.

Following the standard, the Tool Impact (TI)[1] and Tool Error Detection (TD)[2] are to be determined for these tools.

Finally, the Tool Confidence Level (TCL)[3] is used to determine the measures that should be taken to prevent bugs from

---

[1] possibility that a malfunction of a particular software tool will cause or fail to detect errors in a safety-related item or element being developed [38, Req. 11.4.5.2]

[2] confidence in tools, that malfunctions and resulting erroneous output will be prevented or detected [38, Req. 11.4.5.2]

[3] level if the software development tool requires further qualification methods to gain confidence in its results or work products [38, Tab. 3]

being introduced into the software for use in safety-critical applications.

First we look at the TI. In the Figure 8.5 you can see the AI part of the software, which is generated by the software tools, the nodes or algorithms on the one hand, and the parameters of the software on the other.

The Tool Impact is clearly recognisable. The AI has a direct influence on the functionality of the application, **TI2** is to be selected [38, Req. 11.4.5.2].

The determination of Tool Error Detection is, in my opinion, equally clear. The goal of AI frameworks is to achieve predefined prediction accuracies. Therefore, if the targets are met, it can be implicitly assumed that E/E failures[4] in the algorithm or parameterisation can be ruled out.

Finally, performance weaknesses are not considered within the framework of ISO 26262.

This results in a **TD1**, albeit surprisingly. Although the AI frameworks have not been developed to safety standards, this results in a **TCL1**, which means that **no additional qualification methods** need to be applied.

I also come to **TCL1** when evaluating the AI test environment. The tipping point here is again **TD1**, with the same argument as for the development tools. Tests cannot be successfully completed without achieving the specified prediction accuracy.

The assignment of **TD1** to **TCL1** makes it unnecessary, at least for this application, to consider the extent to which the test equipment affects the product and the TI results.

---

[4]   programming failures

WP: Software tool qualification report

If TCL1 cannot be achieved for software tools, measures or justifications are required to increase confidence in the tool. These include, but are not limited to, a high level of maturity, many years of experience with the tool without anomalies or bugs, large user communities in application areas similar to the target application.

Alternatively, the development process of the tools could be evaluated to ensure that they are free of defects. A validation of the software tools by means of a 'golden sample' would also be conceivable, as would a development process for the tools according to a security standard.

However, according to TCL1, no additional methods need to be used to increase trustworthiness.

10.2. Clause 12 - Qualification of software components

The qualification of software components is intended to ensure that software modules not developed in-house, e.g. open source software or commercial off-the-shelf modules, meet the safety requirements according to the assigned ASIL.

Again, I would apply the same reasoning as above. To achieve the target functionality with the desired prediction accuracy, the activation functions, algorithms and parameters must be correct. For me, this rules out E/E errors in the sense of ISO 26262.

Of course, this does not mean that aspects of cybersecurity[5] or safety of the intended functionality[6] do not require other approaches.

WP: Software component documentation

This work product requires documentation of various properties of the software component, such as unique identification of the software component, maximum ASIL of potential security objectives that can be violated by the component, requirements of the component to the host application, and so on.

This is information without AI specific parts, as the AI application can be understood as a fixed library with associated application programming interface (API). Therefore, this work product can be treated in the same way as conventional software components.

WP: Software component qualification report

This work product shall show the test coverage of all requirements relevant to the software component for both normal operation (good testing) and failures (bad testing).

Special attention should be paid to the testing of an unchanged implementation of the software component as well as a complete documentation.

Although specific tools are used to test AI components, the requirements of the work product are no different to those of non-AI applications.

WP: Software component qualification verification report

Similarly, there is no difference between the test report required by this work product [38, 12.4.3] for AI applications and for conventional applications.

11. Conclusion: AI specifics in ISO 26262

Consideration of potentially AI-affected ISO 26262 work products has revealed a picture that is quite surprising to me:

On-board AI applications differ from conventionally programmed applications in only a few aspects.

Specification Machine Learning specifics

The creation of a Item definition requires the development of AI-specific functions and algorithms, their pre-parameterisation[1], training and verification, additional knowledge about Machine Learning and, above all, a precise definition of the learning objective. This requires an addition to the evidence of competencies.

Data provision

Specific to AI applications is the need to provide sufficient and appropriate learning and test data for training and testing. Here, the potentially large amount of data due to permutations of possible data variants is as much a challenge as the qualitatively sufficient pre-treatment of the training and verification data through correct tagging. This requires appropriate processes and tools.

---

[1]   hyperparameter

Distinction between E/E errors and nominal performance

Correctly identifying the not always predictable results of AI as a performance problem and distinguishing them from real E/E errors is another challenge, especially for the creation of the Hazard Analysis and Risk Assessment and Safety goals.

Development process and tools

The process and tool chain for algorithm development, parameterisation and verification need to be complemented by AI frameworks for the software development process and documentation of software tools.

12. EGAS

12.1. EGAS Concept

The Electronic Gas Actuation System principle in ISO 26262 is a framework that guides the design of safety-critical systems in vehicles, emphasising clarity, separation, abstraction and reliability.

Similar to the MECE (Mutually Exclusive, Collectively Exhaustive) principle, Electronic Gas Actuation System (EGAS) ensures that functions are both distinct in their operation and comprehensive in their coverage of safety requirements.

Both principles aim to reduce risk by structuring systems in a clear, non-overlapping way that addresses all necessary safety elements.

The aim is to develop a simple and manageable monitoring system that detects *single and double faults*, including *residual faults*, and leads to *controllable system responses*.

As a development guideline and principle, the aim is to achieve the highest possible system availability, which is to be achieved, among other things, through graduated error reactions and error detection[1] with the corresponding confirmation[2].

Monitoring functions should be kept *robust and simple*, and the effectiveness of redundant shutdown paths should be *checked before each driving cycle*. [20]

---

[1]   error detected

[2]   error confirmed

12.2. Item definition

To provide a suitable framework for the following considerations, here is a fictitious example of an object recognition based emergency braking assistance.

Admittedly, this is not a complete item definition [25], but only the relevant aspects are considered.

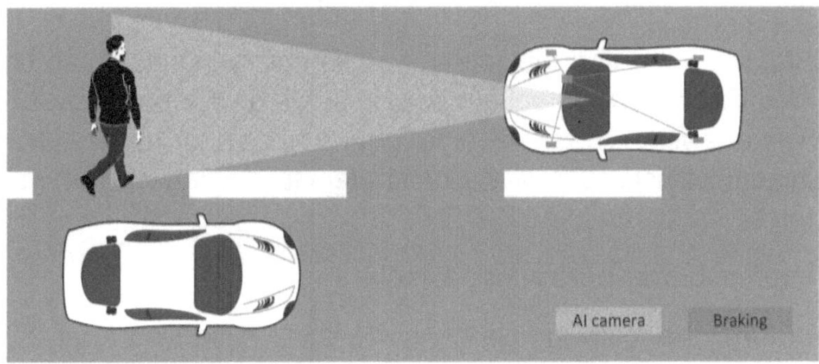

Fig. 12.1.: Item definition - emergency braking assistance

An embedded camera system equipped with object detection will initiate an emergency braking manoeuvre in the braking system via the vehicle bus as soon as people or other obstacles are detected in the lane.

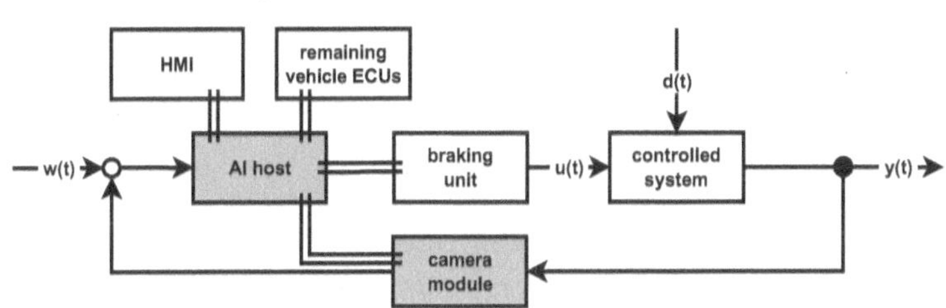

Fig. 12.2.: System overview emergency brake

12.3. Hazard Analysis and Risk Assessment

The following considerations are an adaptation of the EGAS methodology as described in [20, EGAS-80].

This approach provides a structured method for deriving safety objectives from identified hazards, ensuring compliance with safety standards such as ISO 26262.

Based on the Item definition, an exemplary situation can be identified where potential hazards serve as the basis for further analysis. These hazards form the basis for understanding critical risks and mitigation strategies in safety-critical systems.

- running over person or obstacle

In turn, the following Safety goals can be derived from the situations as examples:

- SG 001 - The running over of persons due to malfunctions of the emergency brake assist shall be prevented with ASIL x.

Safety Goal SG 001 necessitates the implementation of a robust monitoring concept. This concept must ensure the reliable *detection of E/E errors* in the recognition of persons and objects. Such detection mechanisms are crucial for identifying malfunctions in emergency brake assist systems, thereby preventing hazardous situations.

The focus on E/E errors is a direct result of applying the principles of ISO 26262 within the EGAS framework. This targeted approach allows for a systematic reduction of risks associated with hardware and software malfunctions, ensuring alignment with functional safety standards. [20, EGAS-87]

12.4. Functional Safety Concept

As the analysis relates to the applicability of the EGAS concept to AI-based systems, I focus on the relevant aspects of the Functional Safety Concept (FSC).

Passing over persons or objects can be triggered from faulty object detection *caused by E/E errors.*

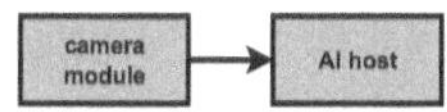

Fig. 12.3.: ECU components

The ECU is distributed into the following components:

- sensor (camera module)
- controller (AI host)

This results in the following safety requirements with ASIL x:

- SREQ 001
  The provision of the sensor signal[3] must be ensured.
  Component: camera module

- SREQ 002
  E/E failures have to be detected[4] and communicated
  Component: camera module

- SREQ 003
  The host system detects failures of the sensor
  Component: AI host

- SREQ 004
  The host system detects E/E failures of the AI host
  Component: AI host

---

[3]   video stream
[4]   self-diagnosis

12.5. Monitoring concept

Based on the components of the ECU[5], the monitoring concept relates only to the AI host.

12.5.1. Level 1 - Functional level

In EGAS, level 1 is understood to be the functional level [20, EGAS-120]. Transferred to the AI application, the functional level represents the analysis of the input data provided to the AI up to the prediction, see '*Nodes, algorithms*' and '*parameters*' in Figure 3.11.

Not included are '*Signal analysis, Pre-processing*' and '*Post-processing, results output and error handling*'.

No monitoring is foreseen at this level.

12.5.2. Level 2 - Function monitoring level

According to [20, EGAS-123], the function monitoring level detects faulty processes in the function, i.e. the content of level 1. Similarly, the triggering of system responses in the event of a fault is added to Level 2.

Important at this level is the clear identification of E/E faults affecting the function, i.e. the AI. The monitoring function should be able to detect interface faults[6], scheduling faults[7] and program or data flow[8] faults[9].

---

[5]   see Figure 12.2 and Figure 12.3

[6]   see [37, Tab. 3 1c] and [20, Fig. 3 and 4] (input signals), data integrity check [7, Fig. 9.2]

[7]   see [37, Tab. 3 1f, 1g; Tab. 4 1h]

[8]   see [20, Fig. 3 and 4]

[9]   see [37, Tab. 4 1g]

E/E errors in the sense of ISO 26262 should result in the non-use of AI predictions in the error response. Therefore, no predictions should be given.

Classical design errors or implementation errors cannot usually be detected directly by a monitoring function as self-diagnosis.

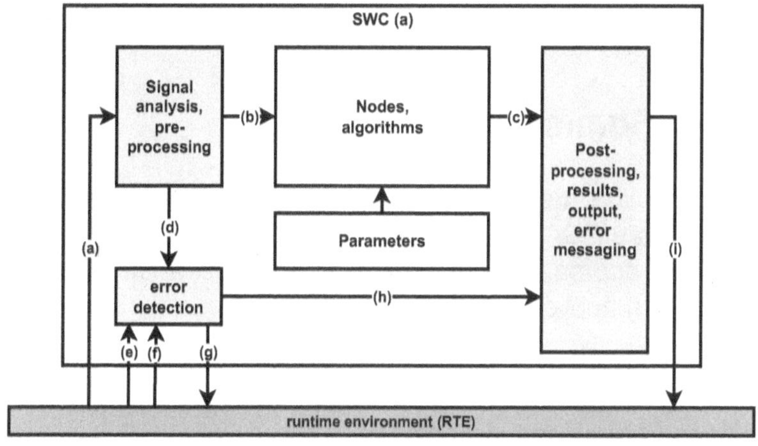

Fig. 12.4.: SWC Level 2 Monitoring

Limitations in the confidence of the AI prediction due to insufficient data quality[10] must be excluded here. These errors would be analysed and treated as performance insufficiencies [41].

12.5.3. Level 3 - Computer monitoring level

Level 3 includes the control of the computing device, e.g. microcontroller or ASIC [20, EGAS-126] for errors and appropriate error responses.

---

[10]   contrast loss due to brightness, fog or lens opacity, i.e. non-E/E errors

The computer monitoring self-diagnoses required for level 3 are not AI specific. AI can be considered as a black box within Software Component (SWC).

Memory errors, sequence errors [7, Fig. 9.2] and errors in the interpretation of instruction sets have to be identified. Also to be diagnosed are HW configuration errors, HW modules running independently, the HW error management [20, EGAS-605].

12.6. Summary

In my opinion, the *3-Level Safety Monitoring (3-LSM)*, also referred to as *EGAS*, proposed by Robert Bosch GmbH, offers a robust approach to implementing *onboard* artificial intelligence (AI) applications[11] in automobiles.

This methodology provides a structured, hierarchical monitoring system capable of addressing safety requirements specific to AI-enabled functionalities.

It is essential to distinguish between traditional *E/E faults*, as defined in ISO 26262, and *performance deficiencies* carried out in ISO 21448.

E/E faults refer to deterministic hardware or software failures that are mitigated by fault detection mechanisms, whereas performance issues refer to the inability of an AI system to perform as expected due to limited training data or unexpected environments.

For example, if the AI system fails to make a prediction due to input data outside its trained domain, this is a performance issue, not a failure. Such cases highlight the need for extensive data coverage and robust validation to mitigate deficiencies.

---

[11]   based on supervised learning

It is important to note that a *prediction rate* should not be confused with a *error rate*.

In the context of AI applications, the prediction rate reflects how often the system can produce a valid output for a given input. This differs from the error rate, which measures the frequency of incorrect outputs when predictions are made.

For practical applications, a reasonable threshold for a tolerable prediction rate needs to be defined. This threshold should take into account both the technical feasibility of achieving high prediction rates and a balanced assessment of risk to ensure that the system remains safe and reliable under real world operating conditions.

Once the AI algorithms have been developed, parameterised and trained within a neural network, the AI component becomes a *static pattern recognition black box* with prediction accuracy verified using *golden sample* datasets. This static nature, where parameters and structure remain fixed, simplifies integration into safety-critical systems.

For *onboard* applications, 3-LSM can monitor AI behaviour in real time. Level 1 monitors raw inputs for anomalies, Level 2 checks outputs against safety thresholds, and Level 3 triggers fallback strategies or safe state transitions as required. This layered approach provides comprehensive safety and reliability.

In summary, the integration of structured safety frameworks such as 3-LSM, combined with rigorous training, validation and a clear distinction between defects and performance issues, supports the reliable and safe use of AI in automotive applications.

Part III.

Cybersecurity

13. Cybersecurity Meets AI

AI and cybersecurity are two areas that have attracted a lot of attention in recent years. Both promise revolutionary solutions, but are often accompanied by a fair share of 'buzzwords' and unrealistic expectations.

When these domains intersect, the challenges multiply and require a clear, structured approach to understanding and addressing their unique intersections.

This chapter lays the groundwork for exploring the process and technical specifics of cybersecurity in the context of AI.

First, we focus on the processual characteristics and challenges of ensuring cybersecurity in AI systems.

We will then delve into the technical analysis of AI-specific cybersecurity threats and attack vectors.

13.1. AI Demands for a Unique Approach to Cybersecurity

AI systems differ significantly from traditional software systems in their design, operation and vulnerabilities.

While traditional cybersecurity focuses on *securing code*, *networks* and *infrastructure*, AI introduces additional dimensions.

DYNAMIC LEARNING BEHAVIOUR AI evolve over time, learning from new data. This dynamic nature creates new vulnerabilities, such as the possibility of data poisoning or adversarial training.

COMPLEXITY AND OPACITY The often opaque 'black-box' nature of AI makes it difficult to predict how the system will respond to specific inputs, leading to potential exploitation by malicious actors.

DEPENDENCE ON DATA The reliance on large data sets for training and operation introduces risks related to data integrity, privacy and provenance.

These factors require a specialised approach to cybersecurity that takes into account the unique properties of AI systems.

13.2. Processual Challenges in AI Cybersecurity

Before diving into the technical details, it is crucial to establish robust processes for identifying and mitigating cybersecurity risks in AI systems.

These processes need to integrate traditional cybersecurity frameworks with AI-specific considerations.

LIFECYCLE MANAGEMENT AI require continuous monitoring and updating, as new vulnerabilities may emerge over time due to changes in the operational environment or the dataset.

This topic is very wide-ranging and is therefore discussed in chapter 'Processual AI Risks' S. 163 is discussed further.

RISK ASSESSMENT Traditional threat modelling must be extended to include AI-specific attack vectors such as model inversion or evasion attacks. This AI specificity will be addressed in the product lifecycle, see 'Manipulation', p. 165.

STAKEHOLDER COLLABORATION Cybersecurity in AI involves multiple stakeholders, including data scientists, software engineers, and cybersecurity experts.

Effective collaboration and communication is key to addressing the challenges comprehensively. However, only AI-specific work products need to be added into existing cybersecurity processes.

13.3. Setting the Stage for Technical Analysis

With a clear understanding of the processual specifics, we can now focus on the technical aspects of cybersecurity in AI systems. This includes identifying and mitigating threats unique to AI, such as adversarial attacks, data poisoning, and model extraction.

These topics will be explored in detail in chapter 'Technical AI Risks' p. 188.

14. Processual AI Risks

The application of AI throughout the product lifecycle has already been described in section 'Process Support for Product Lifecycle', p. 71. When following the product lifecycle, various aspects related to cybersecurity should be considered.

However, I will focus specifically on AI-related aspects and their implications for cybersecurity.

14.1. Idea

At the concept stage, it is important to assess whether implementing a function using AI introduces potential risks from the outset.

Questions should be asked about whether the prediction accuracy is sufficient for the intended application and whether it will satisfy the end user of the function.

Consideration of Non-Deterministic Behaviour

In addition, the possibility of unforeseen effects and risks arising from the use of AI should be carefully considered, such as:

HALLUCINATIONS   AI systems may generate false or misleading results. Causes of AI Hallucinations:

- Insufficient training data
- Overfitting
- Lack of context
- Algorithmic limitations

DISCRIMINATION AND AMPLIFICATION OF BIASES AI systems can unintentionally reinforce societal or algorithmic biases and ethical misbehavior. This occurs because AI systems, particularly machine learning models, often rely on large datasets for training. These datasets may contain inherent biases present in society or reflect historical inequities.

These biases can manifest in AI systems in several ways:

- **Data/Algorithmic Bias**: If the data used to train AI models is not representative of the population or the task it is meant to perform, the AI system is likely to learn and perpetuate those biases[1]. [22]
- **Sampling Bias**: If certain groups are over-represented or under-represented in the training data, AI systems may make inaccurate or unfair predictions[2].
- **Label Bias**: In supervised learning, if the labels in the training data reflect societal prejudices or stereotypes, the AI model may reinforce these biases[3] in its predictions.

The consequences could include the following aspects, which should be considered in the brainstorming phase:

- **Unfair treatment of road users:** AI systems can disadvantage certain groups of road users due to bias in the training data, leading to misclassification or overlooking of pedestrians or cyclists from certain social or ethnic groups. [66, 52]
- **Reinforcement of existing inequalities:** The use of AI in vehicles harbours the risk of reinforcing existing social inequalities. [70]

---

[1] e.g., a facial recognition system trained primarily on images of light-skinned people may fail to recognise people with darker skin tones

[2] e.g., an AI model trained on male medical data may fail to analyse female data

[3] e.g., if the data set used to train an AI model for hiring decisions has labels influenced by gender or age stereotypes, the AI system may inherit and perpetuate these biases

164

- **Safety risks:** A manipulated AI system[4] could deliberately make the wrong decisions, for example to cause an accident. [23, 62]
- **Loss of trust:** If AI is perceived to discriminate, public trust in the technology could be undermined, making autonomous vehicles harder to adopt. [72]
- **Legal consequences:** The integration of AI poses significant challenges for organisations who need to ensure that their AI systems comply with legal requirements[5].
  For users, this means adapting to new forms of mobility and potentially being held liable for accidents or rule-breaking[6] caused by AI errors. [19]

MISINFORMATION   AI models in automotive applications can spread false information[7] or make decisions based on faulty data, which poses significant safety risks.

Misinformation can also come from faulty external data, like incorrect road conditions or misleading vehicle-to-vehicle (V2V) communication. If AI systems rely on such data to make real-time decisions, they may act on false information, resulting in unsafe actions such as taking an incorrect route or misadjusting speed. [18]

MANIPULATION   Adversaries can exploit AI systems to maliciously manipulate outcomes[8]. It could also involve manipulating sensor data, altering V2V communications, or even

---

[4]   e.g., manipulation in deliberate bias of training data, targeted provision of manipulated sensor data

[5]   Legal requirements are rather vague and subject to change as they are influenced by the evolving nature of technology and the current state of knowledge and understanding in both policy and science.

[6]   road traffic regulations, regulatory offences

[7]   can arise from errors in sensor data, biased training datasets, or corrupted inputs

[8]   e.g., by introducing misleading inputs or hijacking data streams that influence decision-making processes

injecting false environmental information, leading to danger-
ous actions or system failures.

PRIVACY VIOLATIONS   AI may inadvertently access, misuse,
or expose personal data[9], leading to significant privacy concerns in automotive applications.

In addition, the flow of training data used to improve AI
models may include personal data that, if not sufficiently
anonymised, could be accessed by external parties, potentially leading to unauthorised profiling or breaches of
confidentiality.

These risks underscore the need for strong data protection
protocols and clear user consent mechanisms to protect privacy. [69, 53]

Challenges of hacking and playfulness

The allure of new technologies presents a tempting challenge
for hackers and users alike, particularly in the area of AI-
driven automotive applications.

The novelty of AI systems, combined with the complexity of
their functionality, often motivates hackers to look for vulnerabilities and exploit unexpected use cases.

This 'playful' behaviour can lead to attempts to influence or
manipulate AI-based functions, such as altering vehicle control systems, bypassing security measures or misdirecting
autonomous decision making. [43, 61]

In addition, the desire to explore new forms of interaction with
AI-powered vehicles can lead to unintended consequences,

---

9   e.g., the collection and processing of driving data, such as location,
     behavioural patterns, and preferences, may inadvertently share this
     data with third parties, such as service providers, insurers, or adver-
     tisers, without appropriate consent or transparency

including security breaches or the creation of new entry points for cyber-attacks.

These challenges highlight the need for robust security measures and continuous testing to anticipate and mitigate potential misuse. [5, 14]

At the end of such considerations, it is always worth asking the somewhat provocative question: Is the use of AI really *necessary or essential* in this context, or is it *simply following a trend* without adding significant value?

14.2. Functional Specification

An extremely important step in AI cybersecurity is already taken at the idea description stage, where potential risks and functional requirements are identified early on.

The functional specification serves as a direct result of this process, ensuring that the derived requirements cover not only functional aspects but also cybersecurity considerations.

AI Error Handling

The functional handling of AI-specific failures shall be given particular attention in the functional specification to ensure that robust mechanisms for detection, handling and communication of failures are clearly defined and effectively integrated into the system.

DETECTION   Identify when the AI system is behaving unexpectedly or incorrectly. This includes specifying AI-based monitoring systems capable of detecting anomalies and potential malfunctions.

TREATMENT   Introduction of confidence factors as indicators of the credibility of predictions for downstream systems, together with fallback mechanisms to deal with uncertain or incorrect predictions.

These measures will ensure continuity of operations and minimise the risks associated with AI errors.

COMMUNICATION   Provide alerts[10] to end users, but also to downstream systems and data receivers.

In addition, schedule and generate detailed log data to support effective troubleshooting and fault analysis, enabling a systematic approach to identifying and resolving faults in the AI system.

Applied Diagnosis

The applied diagnosis of AI applications places extensive demands on the diagnostic specification. It is important to note that only functional aspects are considered here and are included in the functional specification.

DATA QUALITY AND CONSISTENCY

- **Data Validation:** A mechanism shall be established to verify AI parameters[11] for versioning, status, completeness, accuracy and compliance with defined quality standards.
- **Test patterns:** Verifying the predictive ability of the AI using predefined test patterns can be particularly useful, especially when it is difficult to place the vehicle in the required state or scenario during testing.

---

[10]   Integrate fault alerts into the vehicle's warning and display system to ensure clear and intuitive communication of AI-related issues to users.

[11]   see fig. Node cluster parameter set p. 27

- **Consistency Checks:** Reading certificates or hashes of the parameter sets used can help ensure consistency and facilitate debugging.

MODEL PERFORMANCE AND BEHAVIOUR

- **Performance Metrics:** Establish a method for evaluating how effectively computing performance matches the demands of AI algorithms might be helpful. Monitoring processor load and memory usage metrics can provide valuable insight into diagnosing performance issues. [59]
- **Bias Detection:** Collecting historical data and performing statistical analysis can reveal potential biases, providing valuable insight for problem analysis and further development of the AI model.

SECURITY AND PRIVACY

- **Anomaly Detection:** Detecting unusual patterns in traffic or model behaviour that may indicate security breaches is critical to maintaining system integrity.
- **Privacy Breach Detection:** Monitoring the system for potential privacy violations, such as unauthorised access to sensitive data, is essential.
- **Privacy by Design:** Ensuring that privacy measures are integrated throughout the development process is a fundamental requirement.
- **Data Transfer:** A principle of data minimisation should always be observed, particularly in the context of AI. Environmental data, for example, should be assessed in terms of both privacy and the need to collect it.

As can be seen from these initial considerations, the applied diagnosis of AI-based systems is far from trivial and should therefore be approached with caution.

AI Training Data

The cybersecurity requirements for AI training data for automotive systems are extensive and complex. Below are some critical aspects that should be considered and balanced within the functional requirements:

REPRESENTATIVENESS AND DIVERSITY

- **Real world scenarios:** The training data should represent realistic traffic situations, including unpredictable events and exceptions, which are of course maximally dependent on the target functionality. [42, 45]
- **Diversity:** The data should include a wide range of vehicles, road conditions, weather scenarios, and road users to ensure a robust and generalisable AI system. Again, this is driven by the intended functionality.
- **Adversarial Examples:** To increase the AI's resilience to manipulation, adversarial examples - data deliberately designed to mislead the AI - should be included in the training dataset, see 'Adversarial Examples in Machine Learning' p. 192.

QUALITY AND ACCURACY

- **Exact annotations:** The data must be annotated accurately and consistently, as errors or inconsistencies can lead to AI malfunctions. This should be specified in the requirements.
- **Data Cleaning:** The dataset should be cleaned of noise, outliers and redundant information. Depending on the intended functionality and the amount of data required, this may be a hard requirement to specify.
- **Periodicity:** Training data should be updated regularly to ensure that the AI remains at the cutting edge of technology. The AI's generation of training data should also be

evaluated in this context [67]. It could lead to a deterioration in learning outcomes [12].

Criteria for the quality of training data need to be specified to ensure that the AI system works as intended. These specifications should be aligned with cybersecurity standards, both procedurally and content-wise, through intensive review processes. [88]

PRIVACY AND SECURITY

- **Anonymisation:** The strict anonymisation of personal data must also be laid down in the training data. A reference to a transcript of records could not be sufficiently unambiguous, depending on the desired functionality.
- **Encryption:** In the case of continuous learning of the AI, encryption of training data from the field is to be considered.
- **Access control:** Strict access controls, including through the toolchain and AI frameworks used, should be specified to minimise the risk of data breaches.

ROBUSTNESS AGAINST ATTACKS

- **Adversarial Training:** The AI should be trained with adversarial examples to improve its robustness against manipulation. Again, a reference to cross-cutting principles of cybersecurity standards is not sufficient; precise requirements for adversarial examples in the application are necessary.
- **Differential Privacy:** Differential privacy techniques can be used to protect the privacy of individual data points. If privacy-sensitive data is to be used, splitting the training data is one possible means, but it needs to be specified.
- **Security audits:** Training data should be regularly audited for potential security vulnerabilities. The audit criteria should be clear and project specific.

AI-Specific Considerations in the Review Process

The specific characteristics of AI for cybersecurity outlined above lead to specific additional requirements for the review process, as prescribed by various standards.

A key aspect is the increased interdisciplinarity which, in addition to the purely formal aspects of the functional specification, places particular emphasis on the following considerations:

AI AND AI TRAINING The review process must ensure that the AI models and training data are thoroughly evaluated for effectiveness and safety. This includes verifying that the training data is diverse, representative and free from bias, while ensuring that the AI models are able to perform as expected under different conditions.

AI ROBUSTNESS AND ADVERSARIAL TRAINING AI systems must be robust to various types of attack, including adversarial attacks where malicious input is used to fool the model. The verification process must assess the AI system's resilience to such attacks and ensure that adversarial training techniques are incorporated to improve the model's robustness, safety and security. This involves testing the model under adversarial conditions and implementing countermeasures to protect against vulnerabilities.

PRIVACY As AI systems often rely on large amounts of data, including sensitive personal data, it is essential to ensure compliance with data protection regulations (such as GDPR). The review process should focus on how data is collected, processed, stored and shared, ensuring that this is done in a way that protects the privacy and security of individuals.

The review team should therefore include experts in cybersecurity and safety, privacy and ethics, as well as experts in the functionality.

14.3. Technical Specification

The technical specification represents the practical implementation of the functional specification(s), system specification(s) and non-technical specifications. It brings together a wide range of different requirements[12] and objectives to form a coherent framework as a basis for the implementation process.

This involves not only addressing the functional requirements, but also combining them with critical cybersecurity and AI considerations. These aspects must be carefully balanced to ensure both the performance and security of the system.

The following sections provide an overview of the resulting specifications for hardware and software. While key aspects are highlighted, the content does not claim to cover all possible implementation details or edge cases.

14.3.1. Hardware Development

The development of hardware for AI applications in safety-critical systems requires careful consideration of cybersecurity aspects. Key points include:

CYBERSECURITY IN COMPONENT SELECTION Choosing appropriate hardware components, such as Hardware Security Module (HSM), is essential to building security features directly into the hardware.

---

[12]   see also fig. 5.5 Alignment Specifications p. 75

Components with built-in security features, such as tamper detection, encryption engines, and secure key storage, help protect sensitive data[13] and prevent unauthorised access.

These security features are particularly important in systems where data integrity and confidentiality are critical.

In addition, the selection process must consider the overall security of the system, ensuring that all components, particularly AI-specific elements, work together to minimise vulnerabilities.

AVOID EASILY IDENTIFIABLE PATTERNS   The following hint is not necessarily specific to AI. Debug or production interfaces, such as ISP or debug connectors, should not be easily identifiable or accessible to prevent potential attackers from exploiting these interfaces.

These connectors can be entry points for unauthorised access, so it is essential to conceal them or use physical protection methods. This also applies to necessary test points on Printed Circuit Boards (PCBs), which should be designed to make them less accessible to unauthorised personnel.

By ensuring that these points are not easily identifiable, the risk of tampering or reverse engineering is significantly reduced.

COMPONENT SELECTION   Choosing appropriate hardware components, such as HSM, is essential to building security features directly into the hardware. Components with built-in security features, such as tamper detection, encryption engines, and secure key storage, help protect sensitive data and prevent unauthorised access.

These security features are particularly important in systems where data integrity and confidentiality are critical. In addition, the selection process must consider the overall security of the system, ensuring that all components work together to minimise vulnerabilities.

AI-specific hardware, such as AI accelerators and specialized processors, is designed to handle the computational demands of machine learning and AI algorithms. These devices often come with built-in cybersecurity features to ensure the secure execution of AI workloads and the protection of sensitive data.

Some typical cybersecurity features[14] available in AI-specific hardware include:

- Secure Boot
- Hardware Encryption
- Trusted Execution Environment
- Key Management
- Tamper Detection
- Side-Channel Attack Mitigation
- Hardware-accelerated Cryptography

14.3.2. Software Development

The software development for AI applications in safety-critical systems must address both cybersecurity and data protection considerations throughout the entire process:

TOOLS AND DEVELOPMENT ENVIRONMENT

- **Cybersecurity Guidelines:** When selecting development tools and platforms for AI, cybersecurity requirements should be considered to avoid vulnerabilities in the toolchain.

---

[14]   For details, see Glossary p. 212

- **Data Protection During Training:** Data used during AI training must be processed in compliance with data protection regulations, particularly when sensitive or personal data is involved.

SOFTWARE ARCHITECTURE

- **Integration of AI Components:** The software architecture should integrate AI components while adhering to cybersecurity principles, such as clear separation of safety-critical functions from less critical parts.
- **Memory Concepts:** The integrity and protection of AI parameters and related data must be ensured. This includes mechanisms to prevent tampering and secure access to memory.

14.4. Technical Implementation

The technical implementation of AI systems in automotive applications requires a meticulous approach to ensure system reliability, safety, security and compliance with industry standards.

While many considerations are made during the specification phase, the focus here is on the concrete steps taken during the implementation phase.

These include the integration of tools, training frameworks, access control measures and ensuring the overall security of the development and training environment.

TOOLCHAIN INTEGRATION During the implementation phase, particular attention must be paid to the selection and integration of the appropriate toolchain for AI development and training.

AI frameworks such as TensorFlow, PyTorch or others must be evaluated not only for their functionality, but also for their compatibility with the specific requirements of the automotive environment. It is crucial to ensure that the tools chosen support both development and training tasks, enabling seamless workflow and model performance.

ACCESS CONTROL Strict access control to both the tools and the underlying data is essential. Implementing robust mechanisms for managing access ensures that only authorized personnel can interact with sensitive AI development and training tools.

This includes setting up role-based access control (RBAC) to restrict access to critical resources based on the user's role within the organization. Additionally, ensuring that data access is managed securely is paramount to prevent unauthorized data modifications or leaks.

SECURITY OF TRAINING SYSTEMS The systems on which AI models are trained must be secure to prevent tampering and ensure the integrity of the training process.

This includes ensuring that servers and cloud *infrastructure* are protected from potential cyber threats.

Regular system updates and the use of secure communication protocols are essential steps in maintaining the security of these systems.

In addition, vulnerability assessments and penetration tests should be conducted on the hardware and software used for training to identify and mitigate potential vulnerabilities.

VULNERABILITY CHECKS OF TOOLS AND LIBRARIES It is essential that regular vulnerability checks are performed on the tools and libraries used in AI development.

This includes checking for known vulnerabilities in the software components, including the Common Vulnerabilities and Exposures (CVE) databases.

Any tools or libraries with identified vulnerabilities should be either updated or replaced to ensure the system remains secure and compliant with industry standards.

ADHERENCE TO DEVELOPMENT GUIDELINES To maintain high standards of security and quality, AI system development should follow established development guidelines such as MISRA.

These guidelines help to ensure that the AI system meets the necessary safety and performance standards required in automotive applications.

Adherence to such guidelines will minimise the risks associated with software failures and ensure that the AI system is robust, safe and reliable in critical automotive scenarios.

COMPILATION WITH SECURITY AND AI-SPECIFIC SETTINGS Compiling AI software in automotive applications requires specific security measures and consideration of *AI-specific optimisations*:

- Security-oriented compiler options[15]
- AI model execution optimisation
- Error handling and logging

14.5. Verification and Validation

Verification and validation (V&V) play a critical role in ensuring the reliability and security of AI systems, especially in applications where security and privacy are paramount.

---

[15] stack-smashing protection, fstack-protector; Control Flow Integrity (CFI)

This subsection focuses on V&V processes from a cybersecurity perspective, highlighting key issues such as privacy, data quality, red teaming, anomaly detection and compliance with relevant standards.

DATA PROTECTION   In AI systems, data protection is a key concern, particularly when sensitive or privacy-related data is used in testing. Compliance with regulations such as the General Data Protection Regulation (GDPR) is essential.

Access control mechanisms must be in place to ensure that only authorised entities, including third-party service providers, have access to personally identifiable information. Anonymisation of training data can help mitigate privacy risks while still enabling effective model development.

In addition, the AI toolchain needs to be considered to ensure that all components - data collection, preprocessing, training and validation - comply with privacy standards.

Any use of personal data should be done with explicit consent and appropriate safeguards should be put in place to prevent unauthorised access.

DATA QUALITY   The quality of training and validation data has a direct impact on the effectiveness of AI models. Proper labelling (tagging) of data is essential for the training process to ensure that the AI model can learn from accurate and relevant data. In addition, anonymisation of data may be necessary to address privacy concerns.

Furthermore, AI systems need to be rigorously tested to identify potential biases in the training data. Biases can lead to unfair or discriminatory outcomes, which are particularly critical in applications that affect human safety. To avoid these problems, strict separation of training and validation data sets must be enforced to ensure that the validation process remains unbiased.

Furthermore, checking for vulnerabilities such as model poisoning or adversarial attacks during V&V is essential. These security threats can manipulate the behaviour of the model, making it vulnerable to exploitation or incorrect predictions.

RED TEAMING Red teaming involves simulated cyberattacks on AI systems to identify vulnerabilities and weaknesses from a security perspective.

This testing approach helps evaluate how the system would behave under adversarial conditions, ensuring that AI models are resilient to external threats.

Red teams simulate various attack methods, including adversarial attacks and data poisoning, to assess whether the model's behaviour can be manipulated and to identify potential weaknesses in the AI's defences.

Effective red teaming helps to improve the robustness of AI systems, ensuring that they can operate safely in real-world environments.

ANOMALY DETECTION Anomaly detection is critical for identifying deviations in AI system behaviour that may indicate potential security breaches or system malfunctions.

In the context of AI, anomaly detection systems monitor the model's predictions and behaviour to detect unexpected patterns that could indicate adversarial manipulation or errors in the model's performance.

By implementing real-time anomaly detection, AI systems can be continuously monitored to detect anomalous behaviour, such as unexpected predictions or unusual inputs, which may indicate adversarial attacks or data integrity issues. This mechanism helps to maintain the integrity and security of operational AI systems.

CONFORMANCE TO STANDARDS Compliance with standards is an important aspect of the V&V process in AI systems, especially in safety-critical domains. ISO 21434, which focuses on automotive cybersecurity, provides guidelines for ensuring the security of AI systems used in vehicles and other applications.

Compliance with such standards is essential to demonstrate that AI systems meet the necessary safety and cybersecurity requirements.

Ethical considerations should also be incorporated into V&V to ensure that AI systems are developed and deployed in a manner that respects fairness, transparency and accountability.

Ensuring compliance with ethical guidelines and standards helps prevent harmful consequences and ensures that AI systems can be trusted to operate safely in critical environments.

14.6. Production

During the production phase of AI-based systems, several critical aspects need to be carefully managed to ensure security, efficiency, and integration with the broader production environment.

This subsection outlines key considerations for securing data transfer, managing AI learning processes, and raising awareness of cybersecurity and AI applications within production teams.

SECURE DATA EXCHANGE Ensuring secure data transfer between development, production, and the production facility is of paramount importance. This includes not only the direct communication between in-house teams but also incorporating suppliers and subcontractors into the security framework.

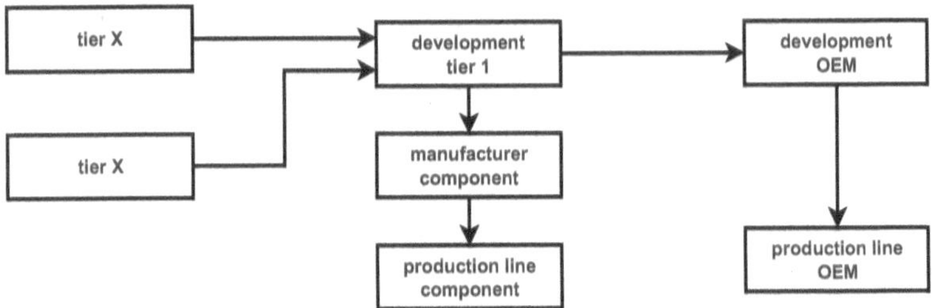

Fig. 14.1.: B2B Data Exchange

All parties involved must adhere to strict security protocols to prevent unauthorized access and data breaches during the transition of AI models, training data, and system updates. Secure communication channels and encryption must be employed to protect sensitive information.

END-OF-LINE PROCESS AND AI LEARNING   The end-of-line process, or the final stage of production, can have significant implications for AI-based learning models.

Changes in the production environment, including hardware variations or discrepancies in sensor data, may affect the performance of AI models that have been trained in controlled environments.

Ideally, these influences should be minimized to avoid disrupting the learning process, which may lead to inaccuracies or model drift.

Where possible, it is crucial to avoid last-minute adjustments that could interfere with AI model performance. Any necessary adjustments should be thoroughly tested in a simulated environment before implementation in production.

RAISING AWARENESS FOR CYBERSECURITY AND AI APPLICATIONS IN PRODUCTION As AI applications become increasingly integrated into production systems, it is essential to raise awareness among production teams about the unique challenges posed by cybersecurity risks and AI-based applications.

Production personnel must be trained to understand the potential vulnerabilities of AI systems, including adversarial attacks and data manipulation risks, as well as the importance of maintaining system integrity. Establishing a culture of awareness and vigilance will help mitigate the risks associated with AI and ensure that production processes are secure and reliable.

14.7. Operation

The operation of AI systems in safety-critical environments requires that end-users are adequately informed about their capabilities, limitations and potential risks. This subsection outlines the key aspects necessary to ensure proper user understanding and interaction with AI-driven systems.

AWARENESS OF INTENDED BEHAVIOUR End-users should be adequately informed about the intended behaviour of the AI system, especially in cases where this behaviour may not be intuitive. Particular emphasis needs to be placed on the 'fuzziness' or probabilistic nature of AI decisions, which may differ from deterministic systems.

INTERVENTION AND LIMITATIONS End-users should be made aware of potential intervention options in AI functionality, such as manual override mechanisms. In addition, they need to understand limitations due to low prediction accuracy, which may result from insufficient or poor quality input or sensor data.

FUNCTIONAL AVAILABILITY It is essential to inform end-users about the availability of the AI system's functionality. This includes clarity about operational conditions that may temporarily limit or suspend certain functionality.

CYBERSECURITY AND DATA PROTECTION Users should be made aware of potential cybersecurity risks, such as adversarial attacks or data breaches, and informed about privacy implications. They should also be given guidance on user-initiated countermeasures, such as restricting access or adjusting system settings, to mitigate these risks.

INTEGRATION IN HUMAN-MACHINE INTERFACES The integration of AI systems into the operational and display concept must provide all necessary information to the user in a clear and accessible manner. This ensures transparency and supports informed decision-making.

CONSIDERATION FOR SECOND-HAND CUSTOMERS Particular attention should be given to second-hand customers, who may not have received the original training or documentation. Ensuring the availability of updated and comprehensive information for these users is necessary for the continued safe operation of AI systems.

14.8. Service

The integration of artificial intelligence applications into safety-critical systems poses unique challenges, particularly in the area of cybersecurity.

This subsection focuses on the cybersecurity aspects of AI applications, with a particular emphasis on service-related issues and responsibilities.

One of the key challenges is the distinction between expected AI behaviour and customer expectations in the field. While AI systems are designed to operate within specific performance parameters, they may occasionally exhibit behaviour that is perceived as anomalous by customers.

Distinguishing these AI performance issues from 'real' repairable failures requires a nuanced understanding of both the design and operational characteristics of the AI system. Misinterpretation of such issues can lead to incorrect fault diagnosis, unnecessary repairs, or missed cybersecurity vulnerabilities.

Another significant challenge arises from the overlap between AI performance issues and cybersecurity concerns. AI systems may underperform due to adversarial attacks or other cyber incidents. Service teams must be able to recognise these scenarios and respond appropriately, ensuring that the system remains functional, safe and secure.

KEY SERVICE RESPONSIBILITIES   The key service responsibilities will be communication and training. Service personnel must be fully trained in two key areas:

- **AI Applications:** Understanding the operating principles, typical behaviours and potential failure modes of AI systems. This knowledge is essential for accurately diagnosing problems and distinguishing between expected behaviour, performance limitations and actual errors.
- **Cybersecurity Aspects:** Recognising and responding to cybersecurity threats that may affect AI systems. This includes awareness of potential attack vectors, mitigation strategies, and recovery processes to maintain system integrity and protect customer data.

ROLE OF EFFECTIVE COMMUNICATION   Effective communication and training will enable service teams to confidently address AI-related challenges, improving both customer satisfaction and system reliability. In addition, continuous feedback loops between service personnel, developers and cybersecurity experts will be essential to refine AI systems and proactively address emerging vulnerabilities.

14.9. Decommissioning

During the decommissioning phase, particular attention should be paid to preventing the theft or misuse of learned data. Data collected during the AI training process, particularly personally identifiable information (PII) or proprietary algorithms, must be securely deleted or anonymised to prevent data breaches. Automatic deletion features could be helpful here.

The system should be thoroughly scrubbed of any sensitive information prior to disposal or repurposing, following established privacy and cybersecurity protocols to ensure compliance with legal and regulatory standards.

All considerations should take into account the technical capabilities of the disposal service provider.

14.10. Implementing AI in the Product Lifecycle

Implementing AI in the product lifecycle is far from being 'just another ugly application'. It requires addressing *unique challenges*, particularly in the area of cybersecurity.

The first step in any AI implementation should always be to assess whether AI is really needed, or whether traditional methods could suffice. This consideration will help *avoid unnecessary complexity* and ensure that the most appropriate solution is chosen.

The unpredictable nature of AI needs to be acknowledged, and this awareness should be integrated throughout the product life cycle (PLC), from design to deployment. AI introduces elements of uncertainty that need to be managed proactively to avoid problems that may arise later in the process.

In addition, AI-specific cybersecurity measures should be combined with classical cybersecurity frameworks, such as those outlined in ISO 21434 and ISO 2700x. This *hybrid approach* ensures that AI applications benefit from both specialised protections and broader, established security practices for automotive and IT systems.

Siloed thinking between development, test, production and service functions *can create vulnerabilities*, so cross-functional collaboration is essential. A holistic view throughout the life-cycle is essential to mitigate risk, ensure robust performance and maintain a secure, reliable system in the face of evolving challenges.

AI should be seen as a useful companion in addressing these challenges, one that can assist in handling complex tasks. However, it must always be monitored and controlled to ensure its actions align with desired goals and standards.

15. Technical AI Risks

In discussions of cybersecurity and artificial intelligence (AI), it is important to identify where AI-specific risks differ from those present in traditional programming paradigms.

So let's take another look at the AI-specific control loop with the cyber security scope.

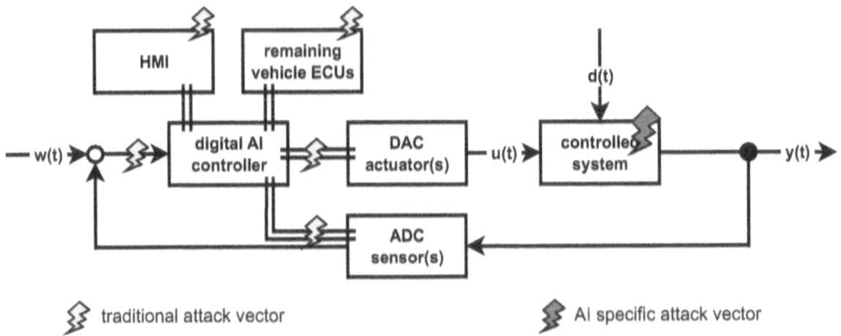

Fig. 15.1.: Attack path' in AI control loop

AI-SPECIFIC CONTROLLER   As discussed in chapter 'Development of AI components' p. 36, the development of AI-specific controllers itself follows the established processes defined in 'Processual AI Risks' p. 163.

The implementation of such controllers is complex but follows traditional programming paradigms. A critical aspect of this is the encapsulation of the AI components within the software, as previously described.

This ensures that the AI functionality is modular and well isolated from other system components.

ACTUATOR CONTROL Actuators, unless they themselves contain AI components, are subject to *traditional development approaches*.

The control information sent to the actuators is derived from the output of the AI digital controller. This output needs to be validated using EGAS methods[1] and should include confidence information to ensure safety and reliability.

With EGAS, actuator control follows *traditional* non-AI.

CONTROLLED SYSTEM While it could previously be assumed that the controlled system 'simply' follows the laws of physics, suddenly aspects of intervention in terms of cybersecurity are added that need to be considered in detail.

The controlled system presents opportunities for attacks in the form of adversarial attacks, particularly evasion attacks.

These types of threats exploit weaknesses in AI models and are discussed in detail in later sections.

SENSOR ATTACKS Attacks that target sensors, provided those sensors do not contain AI components, are *not specific to AI*. Such attacks can and must be detected and mitigated using *traditional methods*, including EGAS. For this reason, sensor-based attacks are not analysed in detail in this chapter.

HUMAN MACHINE INTERFACE (HMI) The Human Machine Interface (HMI) is not an AI-specific component and can be addressed by traditional cybersecurity measures. However, it remains a critical attack vector and must be considered in the broader context of system security. Nevertheless, HMI-specific considerations will not be the focus of this chapter.

---

[1]   see 'Monitoring concept' p. 154

REMAINING VEHICLE ELECTRONIC CONTROL UNITS The remaining vehicle Electronic Control Units (ECUs) can be classified as *traditional attack vectors*.

As these paths are not AI specific, they are excluded from the scope of this analysis. However, their security remains essential to the overall integrity of the system.

15.1. Evasion Attacks in Automotive Applications

15.1.1. Understanding Evasion Attacks

Evasion attacks exploit the vulnerabilities of machine learning models by subtly manipulating input data, including sensitive information from the controlled system, to produce *false outputs without altering the model* itself.

In the context of cybersecurity, such attacks often target the inference phase, bypassing established security mechanisms by creating inputs that fool the model.

For example, a small disturbance in an image can cause a deep learning system to misclassify an object, potentially leading to unsafe behaviour in real-world applications.

15.1.2. Applications in the Automotive World

In automotive systems, evasion attacks pose a significant threat, particularly in scenarios where AI models play a critical role in decision making. Autonomous vehicles rely on AI to process sensor data for navigation, object recognition and environmental understanding.

By introducing adversarial inputs, attackers could cause misinterpretation of *traffic signs, misclassification of objects*, or *incorrect predictions of vehicle trajectories*. Such vulnerabilities highlight the critical importance of robust AI models that can resist evasion attempts.

15.1.3. Affected Sensors in Automotive Systems

Various sensors in modern automotive systems are susceptible to evasion attacks.

CAMERAS The primary target for evasion attacks, as visual data can be easily perturbed to mislead image recognition systems. Examples include adversarial patches on road signs or altered vehicle appearances. [15, 28]

V2V COMMUNICATION Evasion attacks on V2V systems could involve manipulating transmitted data, such as speed or position information, to mislead neighboring vehicles. [10]

VEHICLE-TO-EVERYTHING (V2X) COMMUNICATION Broader than V2V, V2X includes communication with infrastructure[2] and pedestrians. Attackers could manipulate these communications to disrupt decision-making in connected vehicles.

OTHER SENSORS Lidar and radar systems are also vulnerable. Though less common than attacks on cameras, perturbations in these systems' data could still lead to catastrophic errors. [77, 26]

15.1.4. Distinguishing Evasion and Adversarial Attacks

Although evasion attacks are a subset of adversarial attacks, it is important to clarify the differences between them:

---

[2]   e.g., traffic signals, intelligent warning and information signs

EVASION ATTACKS Focus specifically on manipulating input data during the inference phase to evade detection or classification mechanisms. These attacks do not require access to the training process.

ADVERSARIAL ATTACKS A broader category that includes attacks during both the training and inference phases. This includes poisoning attacks, which corrupt the training dataset to introduce vulnerabilities into the AI model.

Understanding this distinction is crucial for implementing targeted defences, as countermeasures for training-based adversarial attacks often differ significantly from those for inference-based evasion attacks.

15.1.5. Conclusion

Evasion attacks pose a significant challenge to the safe use of AI in automotive applications.

By identifying vulnerable sensors and understanding the nature of these attacks, stakeholders can develop robust countermeasures to mitigate risks and enhance the reliability of AI-driven systems. [76]

15.2. Adversarial Examples in Machine Learning

In the field of machine learning, particularly in image recognition, certain images are intentionally crafted to deceive models. These are referred to as *adversarial examples*.

An adversarial example is a data input, often an image, that has been subtly manipulated in such a way that it causes a machine learning model, such as a neural network, to make an incorrect prediction. These manipulations are typically imperceptible to the human eye but are sufficient to confuse the model.

15.2.1. Mechanism of Adversarial Examples

Adversarial examples exploit the fact that machine learning models operate on high-dimensional data spaces. By introducing carefully calculated perturbations to the input data, attackers can shift the model's output significantly. For instance, an image of a cat may be altered by modifying a few pixels, resulting in a model misclassifying it as a dog, while it remains unmistakably a cat to a human observer.

15.2.2. Types of Adversarial Attacks

Adversarial attacks can be categorized into two primary types.

TARGETED ATTACKS The goal is to mislead the model into producing a specific, incorrect output. For example, a model might be tricked into classifying an image of a stop sign as a speed limit sign.

UNTARGETED ATTACKS: Here, the objective is to force the model to produce any incorrect output, without aiming for a specific misclassification.

15.2.3. Implications and Countermeasures

Adversarial examples pose a significant challenge to the robustness and security of machine learning systems, especially in safety-critical applications like autonomous vehicles, medical imaging, and cybersecurity. [50]

Several strategies have been proposed to mitigate these attacks, including:

ADVERSARIAL TRAINING Adversarial training involves augmenting the training dataset with adversarial examples - input data that has been deliberately distorted to exploit model weaknesses.

By exposing the model to these challenging inputs during training, it learns to recognise and resist such manipulations, thereby improving its robustness. This method increases the model's resilience to adversarial attacks and is particularly valuable in critical applications where reliability and security are paramount. [89]

DEFENSIVE DISTILLATION Defensive Distillation uses knowledge distillation techniques to improve the robustness of a model by reducing its sensitivity to adversarial perturbations.

In this approach, a 'teacher' model is used to train a 'student' model, transferring knowledge in a way that smoothes decision boundaries.

This process helps the student model generalise better and resist small, malicious changes to the input data, thereby reducing the effectiveness of adversarial attacks.

Defensive distillation is particularly effective in scenarios that require increased security and stability in machine learning systems. [21]

INPUT PREPROCESSING Input preprocessing involves applying techniques such as noise reduction or feature squeezing to mitigate adversarial interference.

Noise reduction filters out irrelevant data or distortions, while feature squeezing reduces the complexity of the input data by combining similar features. These methods aim to eliminate or neutralise adversarial modifications before they are processed by the model, thereby improving its resilience to attack.

Input preprocessing is a practical and computationally efficient defence strategy, especially for real-time systems that require robust performance. [1]

15.2.4. Conclusion

The exploration of adversarial examples underscores a critical vulnerability in current machine learning models, highlighting their susceptibility to carefully crafted manipulation.

This vulnerability poses significant risks in domains such as autonomous driving, healthcare, and cybersecurity, where accuracy and reliability are paramount. The countermeasures discussed - adversarial training, defensive distillation, and input preprocessing - represent fundamental strategies for strengthening model robustness.

However, the dynamic nature of adversarial techniques requires ongoing research and innovation. Future advances will be critical in developing resilient systems capable of maintaining trust and security in increasingly complex and adversarial environments.

Part IV.

Appendix

Acronyms

A

ADAS Advanced Driver Assistance Systems

AE autoencoder

AI artificial intelligence

ANN artificial neural network

API application programming interface

AR Augmented Reality

ASIC Application Specific Integration Ciruit

AUTOSAR AUTomotive Open System ARchitecture

B

BERT Bidirectional Encoder Representations from Transformers

BSW Basis Software

C

C controllability

C2X Car to X

CFI Control Flow Integrity

CNN convolutional neural network

CVE Common Vulnerabilities and Exposures

D

DFA Dependent failure analysis

E

E	exposure
ECU	Electronic Control Unit
EGAS	Electronic Gas Actuation System
EV	Electric Vehicle

F

F1	F1-score
FET	field effect transistor
FFI	freedom from interference
FMEA	Failure Mode and Effects Analysis
FPGA	field-programmable gate array
FSC	Functional Safety Concept
FTA	Fault Tree Analysis

G

GAN	generative adversarial networks
GDPR	General Data Protection Regulation
GPT	Generative Pretrained Transformer
GPU	Graphics Processing Unit

H

HARA	Hazard Analysis and Risk Assessment
HMI	Human Machine Interface
HSM	Hardware Security Module

I

ID	Item definition
IoT	Internet of Things
ISR	interrupt service routines

K

| **KNN** | K-nearest neighbor |

M

MISRA	Motor Industry Software Reliability Association
ML	Machine Learning
MPU	Memory protection unit

N

NLG	Natural Language Generation
NLP	Natural Language Processing
NN	neural network

O

ODD	Operational Design Domain
OEM	Original Equipment Manufacturer
OTA	Over The Air

P

PaaS	platform as a service
PCA	principal components analysis
PCB	Printed Circuit Board
PII	personally identifiable information

PLC   product life cycle

PNN   physical neural network

R

RBAC   role-based access control

ReLU   Rectified Linear Unit

RL   Reinforcement Learning

RNN   recurrent neural network

S

S   severity

SBOM   Software Bill of Material

SG   Safety goal

Siri   Speech Interpretation and Recognition Interface

SNN   simulated neural network

SoC   System on Chip

SVD   singular value decomposition

SVM   support vector machines

SWC   Software Component

T

TCL   Tool Confidence Level

TD   Tool Error Detection

TEE   Trusted Execution Environment

TI   Tool Impact

TPU   Tensor Processing Unit

V

V2V	vehicle-to-vehicle
V2X	vehicle-to-everything
VPU	Vision Processing Unit

W

| **WP** | work product |

Glossary

A

activation

mathematical function that determines whether a node or neuron passes on the results calculated from the input information to the subsequent nodes or neurons; examples: Sigmoid, ReLU, tanh [29]

application programming interface

interface that enables different software applications to communicate with each other and exchange information

artificial intelligence

Branch of computer science in which an attempt is made to achieve intelligent behaviour of machines by means of algorithms.

A distinction is made between **weak** and **strong** AI.

Weak AI requires human intervention in setting the learning parameters. Typical examples of weak AI are Speech Interpretation and Recognition Interface (Siri), ChatGBT, **autonomous driving**.

Strong AI is currently purely speculative. Examples of this super AI would be Data (character from Star Trek) . [81]

artificial neural network

see NN

autoencoder

unsupervised machine learning method in which two NNs, encoder and decoder, learns to represent input data as efficiently as possible and also to reconstruct it from its compressed form;

mainly used for anomaly detection, localisation tasks [65]

B

Basis Software

Standardised software components for operating the microcontroller, controlling internal and external communication interfaces, as well as other system functions, such as diagnostics, cryptography, end-to-end security. Keyword: Autosar

batch size

hyperparameter that determines how many examples of training data are required to change a weighting

Bidirectional Encoder Representations from Transformers

powerful natural language processing model that develops bidirectional understanding of words and sentences by taking into account the context before and after a word, improving many Natural Language Processing (NLP) tasks

C

Car to X

any off board communication [41, Annex D.4]

Common Vulnerabilities and Exposures

system for identifying and cataloging publicly known cybersecurity vulnerabilities in software and hardware, providing a unique identifier for each vulnerability to facilitate sharing of information

configuration data

Configuration data are **static, pre-configured parameters**[3] for algorithm **within** a Software Component or sub-functions of the Software Component, see Figure 15.2. They are therefore part of the runnables and are accordingly **compiled together with the algorithm**.

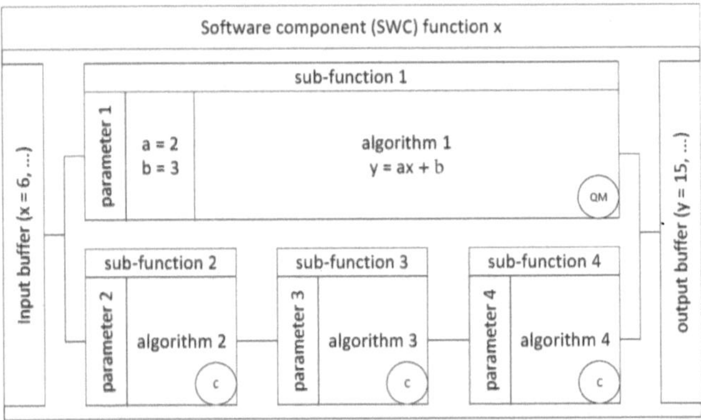

Fig. 15.2.: Configuration data explaination

Typical configuration data are:

- static controller[4] or communication[5] parameters
- ECU identification data (documentation[6])
- border values, limits
- parameterisation of microcontrollers or peripherical components
- trained static parameters if applicable[7] for machine learning algorithms

---

[3]   e.g. non-vehicle specific parameters, parameters for ML algorithm

[4]   e.g. microcontroller settings, fuses

[5]   e.g. SPI communication parameters, CAN dbc, FIBEX

[6]   e.g. serial numbers, HW versions, SW versions, number of production line

[7]   With trained parameters of AI algorithms, only limited statements can be made. It should be considered whether or how faulty patterns can

controllability

possibility for an involved person to get a hazardous situatation under control; rating based on studies or assumptions [41, Req. 6.3]

convolutional neural network

algorithm for convolution operations to capture spatial structures in data

cybersecurity

manipulation of E/E systems for non-intended use using the vehicle infrastructure as well as environments

D

data poisoning

type of adversarial attack where malicious actors manipulate training data to degrade the performance or cause misbehavior in machine learning models. It can target model integrity or availability, often by introducing biased or incorrect data into the training process

deadlock

Programme state in which a task waits indefinitely for the fulfilment of a condition that cannot be fulfilled and thus consumes shared resources.

deductive analysis

drop down analysis, see FTA

Dependent failure analysis

failure analysis technique that identifies and examines the interdependencies between different failure modes in a system;

helps to understand how a failure in one component may propagate and influence other parts of the system, which is crucial for assessing overall system reliability and safety

see [39, Cl.7]

dropout rate

regularization technique used in neural networks where a percentage of neurons are randomly 'dropped out' (set to zero) during training;

helps preventing overfitting by ensuring that the network does not rely too heavily on any single neuron, encouraging more robust learning;

dropout rate typically ranges from 0.2 to 0.5, controlling how many neurons are deactivated at each step

E

exposure

probability of a situation occurring

F

---

be detected, e.g. a quota of areas with '00' or 'FF' over the respective parameter set.

F1-score

is a widely used metric in AI to evaluate the performance of classification models. It considers both precision and recall, providing a balanced measure, especially for imbalanced datasets.
It is defined as:

$$F1 = 2 \cdot \frac{\text{Precision} \cdot \text{Recall}}{\text{Precision} + \text{Recall}}$$

Where:

- **Precision** (*positive predictive value*) measures how many of the instances predicted as positive are actually correct.
- **Recall** (*sensitivity*) measures how many of the actual positive instances were correctly predicted.

In AI applications, the F1 score is particularly useful when the costs of false positives and false negatives are different, or when the dataset is skewed. The score ranges from 0 (worst) to 1 (best).

Failure Mode and Effects Analysis

method

Fault Tree Analysis

method ; Starting from safety/security goals, all paths that lead to a breach of the goals are analysed, drop-down-analysis.

field-programmable gate array

type of integrated circuit that can be reconfigured after manufacturing to perform specific tasks; offers flexibility and customization by allowing users to program its internal logic circuits to suit their desired applications; software defined hardware

freedom from interference

Proof for that they do not influence each other in the aspects of timing and execution[8], memory[9] and exchange[10] of information; see , , , , , FFI

fstack-protector

compiler option used to enhance program security by detecting and preventing stack buffer overflows. It works by placing 'canary' values on the stack to detect any buffer overflow and terminate the program before any malicious code can be executed; option is commonly used in C and C++ programming to mitigate security risks, particularly in the context of systems programming and applications susceptible to buffer overflow vulnerabilities

---

[8] e.g. blocking of execution, deadlocks, incorrect allocation of execution time

[9] e.g. corruption of content, incorrect access to memory used by another software element

[10] e.g. loss, repetition, delay, insertion, incorrect sequence, corruption, masquerade

Functional Safety Concept

work product ISO 26262

G

generative adversarial networks

class of an unsupervised machine learning framework developed by Ian Goodfellow where two neural networks, a generator and a discriminator, perform a zero-sum game in the way of evolutionary race;
mainly used for semantic image editing, style transfer, image synthesis, image and classification [4]

Generative Pretrained Transformer

powerful language model based on the Transformer architecture and trained in advance on large text corpora to solve natural language processing tasks and generate text

global data faults

software fault regarding freedom from interference; measures: cyclic verification of space between memory markers (pattern based); double inverse storage concepts; memory-efficiant checksums; usage of global data faults

Graphics Processing Unit

specialized electronic circuit that accelerates graphics and visual data processing, commonly used in gaming, computer graphics, and other applications that require high-performance calculations; can be used for AI

H

Hardware Encryption

provides on-chip encryption capabilities for secure data storage and transmission, ensuring that sensitive information is protected from unauthorized access

hardware register faults

software fault regarding freedom from interference; measures: locks for selected configuration registers if applicable, cyclic check current hardware state, periodical rewriting register states (assuming single bit flips as fault model), usage of Memory protection unit

Hardware Security Module

dedicated hardware device for securely performing cryptographic operations, protecting keys, and ensuring data integrity and confidentiality

Hardware-accelerated Cryptography

Hardware units that accelerate cryptographic operations, such as encryption and decryption, providing fast and efficient security processing, crucial for data protection in AI systems

harm

physical injury or damage to the health of persons [34, Req. 3.74]

hierarchical clustering

unsupervised machine learning clustering strategy using tree-like mor-
phologies to cluster datasets and thus create a hierarchy of clusters [68]

Human Machine Interface

Collection of all display and control elements, both hardware and virtu-
alised

hyperparameter

(initial) configuration setting of an AI algorithm, which must be defined
before the learning process begins; not to be confused with model parameters; contains, among other things, learning rate, regularisation
strength number of hidden layers and batch size; see regularisation,
batch size

I

inductive analysis

buttom up analysis, see Failure Mode and Effects Analysis

inference phase

phase in which a trained machine learning model is applied to new input
data to generate predictions or decisions; operates without modifying
the model's parameters and is often deployed in real-time applications;
phase is particularly vulnerable to attacks such as adversarial or evasion
attacks

interrupt faults

software fault regarding freedom from interference; measures: cyclic
check if QM parts disable ASIL parts, higher priority to ASIL interrupt
service routines compared to QM , comparison of QM rate to expected
rate (feature)

Item definition

Description of the function to be developed as comprehensive as possible in a language that is easy to understand; takes into account application scenarios and possible degradation

K

K-means

iterative unsupervised machine learning algorithm to separate data into
non overlapping cluster by using the arithmetic mean [17];
mainly used for structuring data, health care, cluster-than-predict approaches, image compression

K-nearest neighbor

non-parametric supervised machine learning method by Evelyn Fix,
Joseph Hodges and Thomas Cover [44];
mainly used for simple , pattern recognition, data mining, financial
marked predictions, intrusion detection [86]

Key Management

Hardware-based key management solutions for securely generating, storing, and using cryptographic keys, preventing exposure to external threats

L

less reliable QM data quality

software fault regarding freedom from interference; measures: plausibility checks, E2E (feature)

linear regression

supervised machine learning model which finds the linear relationship between dependent and independent variables;

two types are existing, simple linear regression and multiple linear regression;

mainly used for financial risk assessment, business insights, market analysis [55] [60]

logistic regression

supervised machine learning model which finds the linear relationship between dependent and independent variables;

two types are existing, simple linear regression and multiple linear regression;

mainly used for medicine, credit scoring, hotel booking, gaming, text editing [55] [60]

M

Memory protection unit

mechanisms that control access to memory, ensuring that only authorized processes or cores can access specific memory regions, thereby preventing unauthorized data access

Motor Industry Software Reliability Association

organization that develops guidelines for writing safe and reliable software, particularly for embedded systems in the automotive industry; MISRA coding standards, such as MISRA C, aim to ensure software quality and safety by minimizing the risk of errors and vulnerabilities in critical systems

N

Naïve Bayes

supervised machine learning classification approach based on Bayes' theorem [11];

mainly used for text classification, spam detection, and recommendation systems [85]

neural network

represent a physical or virtual recreation of the structure of the human brain with an input layer, one or more hidden layers and an output layer,

where each node (neuron) in each layer is connected to another. When
the output of a node reaches a threshold, it is activated and sends data
to the next layer of the network. Without activation, there is no output.
[82] see also ANN, SNN, PNN

O

Operational Design Domain
conditions for the availability of the automated driving system in its intended design [41, Req. 3.21]

Over The Air
method for software updates via mobile data communication

P

personally identifiable information
data that can identify an individual, such as names, addresses, or identification numbers, requiring protection under privacy laws; see ISO/IEC
29100; PII principal

physical neural network
ADALINE (Adaptive Linear Neuron) by Bernard Widrow and Ted Hoff
electrochemical memristors (memory resistors);
Analog VLSI by Carver Mead using field effect transistors (FETs);
Physical Neural Network by Alex Nugent using nanoparticles, nanowires;
Phase change neural network by Standford Ovshinsky using phase
change material;
Memristive neural network by Greg Snider using memristors (memory
resistors) [57];
see also neural network (NN)

platform as a service
cloud computing service model where a provider offers a platform to develop, deploy, and manage applications without the need to worry about
underlying infrastructure

principal components analysis
unsupervised machine learning method for dimensionality reduction by
removing correlated features and reduction of overfitting;
mainly used for visualisation of multidimensional data, health care,
image resizing, financial stock analyses and forecast returns, pattern
recognition in high-dimensional data sets [58] ; see also singular value
decomposition (SVD)

R

random forest
supervised machine learning algorithm for classification and regression
tasks by combining different decision trees to make best possible decisions [32];
mainly used for health care, finance and banking, stock market, E-
commerce [27]

Rectified Linear Unit

activation function, see activation [29]

regularisation

hyperparameter which shall prevent overfitting of AI models by constraints or penalties during training

S

Secure Boot

ensures that the device starts up only with trusted firmware, preventing the execution of malicious code during the boot process

severity

measure of physical disability of an involved person in the event of S

Side-Channel Attack Mitigation

protection mechanisms designed to prevent attacks that exploit physical side effects (such as power consumption or electromagnetic emissions) to extract sensitive information

simulated neural network

see NN

singular value decomposition

unsupervised machine learning method to perform principal components analysis (PCA) [3][30]

Software Bill of Material

comprehensive list of all the components, libraries, and dependencies included in a software product; provides transparency into the software's structure and helps in identifying vulnerabilities, managing licenses; ensuring compliance with security standards; important for cybersecurity and regulatory compliance, such as in ISO 21434 and other safety standards; enable organizations to track and manage risks associated with third-party software components

stack fault

software fault regarding freedom from interference; measures: stack range check, which checks, wheather the current stack pointer is within the range of allocated stack memory; checking memory markers (feature), usage of Memory protection unit

T

Tamper Detection

monitors the hardware for signs of physical tampering, triggering security responses such as wiping stored data or locking down access to the system

timing and execution faults

software fault regarding freedom from interference; measures: hardware or software watchdogs, supervision of the pogram flow in combination with time stamps (feature)

Tool Confidence Level

level if the software development tool requires further qualification methods to gain confidence in its results or work products [38, Tab. 3]
- TCL1 - no forther qualification methods needed
- TCL2 - qualification methods needed, see [38, Tab. 4]
- TCL3 - qualification methods needed, see [38, Tab. 5]

Tool Error Detection

confidence in tools, that malfunctions and resulting erroneous output will be prevented or detected [38, Req. 11.4.5.2]
- TD1 - high degree of confidence
- TD2 - medium degree of confidence
- TD3 - all other cases, no confidence

Tool Impact

possibility that a malfunction of a particular software tool will cause or fail to detect errors in a safety-related item or element being developed [38, Req. 11.4.5.2]
- TI1 - no impact to safety related item
- TI2 - all other cases

Trusted Execution Environment

secure area within the processor that runs sensitive code in isolation, providing protection against unauthorized access and ensuring that data is processed securely

W

work product

process input and/or output; can be either element of the project goal or documentation

Index

Bibliography

[1] CSCS '19. "Big Automotive Data Preprocessing: A Three Stages Approach". In: *Proceedings of the 2019 Conference on Smart Computing*. 2019. URL: https://orbilu.uni.lu/handle/10993/40415.

[2] *Adaptive Platform AUTOSAR*. URL: https://www.autosar.org/standards/adaptive-platform.

[3] Mohamed Afham. *Singular Value Decomposition and its applications in Principal Component Analysis*. Medium. May 19, 2020. URL: https://towardsdatascience.com/singular-value-decomposition-and-its-applications-in-principal-component-analysis-5b7a5f08d0bd.

[4] Hamed Alqahtani, Manolya Kavakli-Thorne, and Gulshan Kumar. "Applications of Generative Adversarial Networks (GANs): An Updated Review". In: *Archives of Computational Methods in Engineering* 28.2 (Mar. 2021), pp. 525–552. ISSN: 1134-3060, 1886-1784. DOI: 10.1007/s11831-019-09388-y. URL: http://link.springer.com/10.1007/s11831-019-09388-y.

[5] Laura Anderson and Mark Davis. "Vulnerabilities in AI-based Automotive Systems: A Hacking Perspective". In: *Automotive Cybersecurity Review* 8.2 (2020), pp. 75–84. DOI: 10.1007/s10922-020-00523-4.

[6] Martin Arjovsky, Soumith Chintala, and Léon Bottou. *Wasserstein GAN*. 2017. arXiv: 1701.07875 [stat.ML].

[7] Ashraf Armoush. "Design patterns for safety-critical embedded systems". Aachen, Techn. Hochsch., Diss., 2010. PhD thesis. Aachen, 2010, XIV, 181 S. : graph. Darst. URL: https://publications.rwth-aachen.de/record/51773.

[8] *Artificial Intelligence Algorithms For Beginners*. Edureka. July 2, 2019. URL: https://www.edureka.co/blog/artificial-intelligence-algorithms/.

[9] Verband der Automobilindustrie. *VDA 702 Situation catalog E-Parameter as per ISO 26262-3:2018*. Verband der Automobilindustrie, 6/2023. URL: https://webshop.vda.de/VDA/de/vda-702-062023-v2-en.

[10] Mahdi Bagheri et al. "Towards Secure V2X Communication: Evaluating the Impact of Adversarial Attacks". In: *2021 IEEE Vehicular Networking Conference (VNC)*. 2021, pp. 1–6. DOI: 10.1109/VNC52830.2021.9703134.

[11]   *Bayes' theorem*. In: *Wikipedia*. May 8, 2023. URL: `https://en.wikipedia.org/w/index.php?title=Bayes%27_theorem&oldid=1153748919`.

[12]   Emily M Bender et al. "On the Dangers of Stochastic Parrots: Can Language Models Be Too Big?" In: *Proceedings of the 2021 ACM Conference on Fairness, Accountability, and Transparency* (2021), pp. 610–623.

[13]   *Bestärkendes Lernen*. In: *Wikipedia*. Feb. 22, 2023. URL: `https://de.wikipedia.org/w/index.php?title=Best%C3%A4rkendes_Lernen&oldid=231146252`.

[14]   Jack Brown. "Common Attack Methods in AI-Driven Automotive Systems". In: *2024 IEEE Conference on Automotive Cybersecurity*. IEEE. San Francisco, 2024, pp. 101–110. DOI: `10.1109/AutoSec.2024.3456789`.

[15]   Xiaochen Cao et al. "Adversarial Objects Against LiDAR and Camera-based Perception in Autonomous Driving". In: *Advances in Neural Information Processing Systems (NeurIPS)*. 2019.

[16]   Tu Chengsheng, Liu Huacheng, and Xu Bing. "AdaBoost typical Algorithm and its application research". In: *MATEC Web of Conferences* 139 (Jan. 2017), p. 00222. DOI: `10.1051/matecconf/201713900222`.

[17]   Imad Dabbura. *K-means Clustering: Algorithm, Applications, Evaluation Methods, and Drawbacks*. Medium. Sept. 27, 2022. URL: `https://towardsdatascience.com/k-means-clustering-algorithm-applications-evaluation-methods-and-drawbacks-aa03e644b48a`.

[18]   Paul Davis and Olivia Harris. "AI and the Spread of Misinformation in Autonomous Driving Systems". In: *Journal of Cybersecurity and AI* 19.1 (2022), pp. 25–40. DOI: `10.1080/jca.2022.123456`.

[19]   Robert Davis. *Artificial Intelligence and Law in the Automotive Industry*. A comprehensive book exploring the intersection of AI technologies and legal frameworks in the automotive sector. Berlin: Springer, 2022. ISBN: 978-3-030-12345-6. URL: `https://www.springer.com/gp/book/9783030123456`.

[20]   Arbeitskreis EGAS. *Standardisiertes E-Gas Überwachungskonzept für Benzin und Diesel Motorsteuerungen*. July 8, 2015.

[21]   et al. Ge. "Defensive Distillation for Backdoor Removal via Neural Behavior Alignment". In: *Cybersecurity* (2021).

[22]   Lukas Geiger, Laura R. Henke, and Stefan Karle. "Algorithmic Bias in Autonomous Vehicles: Ethical Implications and Challenges". In: *Proceedings of the 2020 IEEE International Conference on Robotics and Automation*. IEEE, 2020, pp. 2155–2162. DOI: `10.1109/ICRA40940.2020.9197132`. URL: `https://ieeexplore.ieee.org/document/9197132`.

[23]   Aaron Gerlach, Brian Binns, and Julian Barrett. "AI Safety Risks Beyond Autonomous Driving: Implications for Automotive Systems". In: *IEEE Transactions on Vehicular Technology* 69.4 (2020), pp. 4620–4629. DOI: `10.1109/TVT.2020.2976887`. URL: `https://ieeexplore.ieee.org/document/8956983`.

[24]   Alex Graves, Abdel-rahman Mohamed, and Geoffrey Hinton. "Speech recognition with deep recurrent neural networks". In: *2013 IEEE International Conference on Acoustics, Speech and Signal Processing*. 2013, pp. 6645–6649. DOI: `10.1109/ICASSP.2013.6638947`.

[25]   Andy Gudera. "Item Definition - Importance of an underestimated Work Product". In: Berlin: tredition GmbH, 2024. ISBN: 978-3-384-32406-1.

[26]   Amira Guesmi and Ihsen Alouani. "Adversarial Attack on Radar-based Environment Perception Systems". In: *arXiv* (2022). Diese Arbeit untersucht, wie adversarielle Angriffe auf UWB-basierte Umgebungswahrnehmungssysteme in autonomen Fahrzeugen durchgeführt werden können, um die Objekterkennung zu stören. Besondere Aufmerksamkeit gilt der Einspeisung von fehlerhaften Signalen zur Beeinflussung der Radarerkennung. URL: `https://ar5iv.labs.arxiv.org/html/2211.01112`.

[27]   *Guide to Random Forest Classification and Regression Algorithms*. Serokell Software Development Company. URL: `https://serokell.io/blog/random-forest-classification`.

[28]   Zuxuan He et al. "Camou: Learning Physical Vehicle Camouflage to Adversarially Attack Detectors in the Wild". In: *International Journal of Computer Vision* 128.6 (2020), pp. 1501–1519.

[29]   *How to Choose an Activation Function for Deep Learning - MachineLearningMastery.com*. URL: `https://machinelearningmastery.com/choose-an-activation-function-for-deep-learning/`.

[30]   Jonathan Hui. *Machine Learning — Singular Value Decomposition (SVD) & Principal Component Analysis (PCA)*. Medium. Jan. 10, 2023. URL: `https://jonathan-hui.medium.com/machine-learning-singular-value-decomposition-svd-principal-component-analysis-pca-1d45e885e491`.

[31] International Organization for Standardization. *ISO 21434:2021 - Road vehicles – Cybersecurity engineering*. International Standard. 2021. URL: `https://www.iso.org/standard/70918.html`.

[32] *Introduction to Random Forest in Machine Learning*. Engineering Education (EngEd) Program | Section. URL: `https://www.section.io/engineering-education/introduction-to-random-forest-in-machine-learning/`.

[33] *ISO 26262-2:2018, Road vehicles - Functional safety - Part 01: Vocabulary*. URL: `https://www.iso.org/obp/ui/#iso:std:iso:26262:-1:ed-2:v1:en`.

[34] *ISO 26262-2:2018, Road vehicles - Functional safety - Part 02: Management of functional safety*. URL: `https://www.iso.org/obp/ui/#iso:std:iso:26262:-2:ed-2:v1:en`.

[35] *ISO 26262-2:2018, Road vehicles - Functional safety - Part 03: Concept phase*. URL: `https://www.iso.org/obp/ui/#iso:std:iso:26262:-3:ed-2:v1:en`.

[36] *ISO 26262-2:2018, Road vehicles - Functional safety - Part 05: Product development at the hardware level*. URL: `https://www.iso.org/obp/ui/#iso:std:iso:26262:-5:ed-2:v1:en`.

[37] *ISO 26262-2:2018, Road vehicles - Functional safety - Part 06: Product development at the software level*. URL: `https://www.iso.org/obp/ui/#iso:std:iso:26262:-6:ed-2:v1:en`.

[38] *ISO 26262-2:2018, Road vehicles - Functional safety - Part 08: Supporting processes*. URL: `https://www.iso.org/obp/ui/#iso:std:iso:26262:-8:ed-2:v1:en`.

[39] *ISO 26262-2:2018, Road vehicles - Functional safety - Part 09: Automotive safety integrity level (ASIL)-oriented and safety-oriented analyses*. URL: `https://www.iso.org/obp/ui/#iso:std:iso:26262:-9:ed-2:v1:en`.

[40] *ISO 26262-2:2018, Road vehicles - Functional safety - Part 10: Guidelines on ISO 26262*. URL: `https://www.iso.org/obp/ui/#iso:std:iso:26262:-10:ed-2:v1:en`.

[41] *ISO/PAS 21448:2019(en), Road vehicles — Safety of the intended functionality*. ISO. URL: `https://www.iso.org/cms/render/live/en/sites/isoorg/contents/data/standard/07/09/70939.html`.

[42] V. John et al. "Saliency Map Generation by the Convolutional Neural Network for Real-time Traffic Light Detection Using Template Matching". In: *IEEE Transactions on Computational Imaging* 1.3 (2015), pp. 159–173. DOI: `10.1109/TCI.2015.2460131`.

[43]   Emily Johnson. *Artificial Intelligence and Playfulness in Automotive Design*. 1st ed. Berlin: TechPress, 2020. ISBN: 978-3-16-148410-0.

[44]   *k-nearest neighbors algorithm*. In: *Wikipedia*. May 8, 2023. URL: `https://en.wikipedia.org/w/index.php?title=K-nearest_neighbors_algorithm&oldid=1153790564`.

[45]   C. Katrakazas et al. "Real-time Motion Planning Methods for Autonomous On-road Driving: State-of-the-art and Future Research Directions". In: *Transportation Research Part C: Emerging Technologies* 60 (2015), pp. 416–442. DOI: `10.1016/j.trc.2015.09.011`.

[46]   Doug Laney. "3D Data Management: Controlling Data Volume, Velocity, and Variety". In: *Gartner Research* (2012). In diesem Artikel beschreibt Laney, wie Unternehmen die 3V-Modelle von Big Data anwenden können, um Daten effektiv zu verwalten.

[47]   Y. Lecun et al. "Gradient-based learning applied to document recognition". In: *Proceedings of the IEEE* 86.11 (1998), pp. 2278–2324. DOI: `10.1109/5.726791`.

[48]   *Machine learning*. In: *Wikipedia*. May 16, 2023. URL: `https://en.wikipedia.org/w/index.php?title=Machine_learning&oldid=1155068763`.

[49]   *Machine Learning Guide for Oil and Gas Using Python*. Elsevier, 2021. ISBN: 9780128219294. DOI: `10.1016/C2019-0-03617-5`. URL: `https://linkinghub.elsevier.com/retrieve/pii/C20190036175` (visited on 11/11/2024).

[50]   Yasas Mahima, Mohamed Ayoob, and Guhanathan Poravi. "Adversarial Attacks and Defense Technologies on Autonomous Vehicles: A Review". In: *Applied Computer Systems* 26 (Dec. 2021), pp. 96–106. DOI: `10.2478/acss-2021-0012`.

[51]   John McCarthy et al. "A Proposal for the Dartmouth Summer Research Project on Artificial Intelligence, August 31, 1955". In: *AI Magazine* 27.4 (Dec. 2006), p. 12. DOI: `10.1609/aimag.v27i4.1904`. URL: `https://ojs.aaai.org/aimagazine/index.php/aimagazine/article/view/1904`.

[52]   Eldon E. McLean and Jason N. Hughes. "Discrimination and Bias in Self-Driving Cars: A Review". In: *IEEE Transactions on Artificial Intelligence* 1.3 (2020), pp. 221–231. DOI: `10.1109/TAI.2020.3001123`.

[53] Sarah Miller and Robert Johnson. "Automotive AI and Privacy Concerns: A Review of Privacy Violations". In: *Proceedings of the International Conference on AI and Privacy*. Berlin, Germany: Springer, 2022, pp. 112–120. DOI: `10.1007/978-3-030-81200-5_15`. URL: `https://link.springer.com/chapter/10.1007/978-3-030-81200-5_15`.

[54] *Mit Reinforcement Learning auf dem Weg zur Allgemeinen KI*. Digitale Welt. URL: `https://digitaleweltmagazin.de/mit-reinforcement-learning-auf-dem-weg-zur-allgemeinen-ki/`.

[55] *ML | Linear Regression vs Logistic Regression*. GeeksforGeeks. Feb. 5, 2020. URL: `https://www.geeksforgeeks.org/ml-linear-regression-vs-logistic-regression/`.

[56] Todd Mummert et al. *What is reinforcement learning?* IBM Developer. URL: `https://developer.ibm.com/what-is-automated-ai-for-decision-making`.

[57] *Physical neural network*. In: *Wikipedia*. Jan. 3, 2023. URL: `https://en.wikipedia.org/w/index.php?title=Physical_neural_network&oldid=1131211637`.

[58] *Principal Component Analysis in Machine Learning | Simplilearn*. Simplilearn.com. URL: `https://www.simplilearn.com/tutorials/machine-learning-tutorial/principal-component-analysis`.

[59] Satyanarayan Raj et al. "AI Workload Analysis and Optimization". In: *ACM Transactions on Computing Systems* 41.4 (2023).

[60] Victor Roman. *Supervised Learning: Basics of Linear Regression*. Medium. Apr. 17, 2021. URL: `https://towardsdatascience.com/supervised-learning-basics-of-linear-regression-1cbab48d0eba`.

[61] M. Rosemberg, J. Mohr, and T. K. Kim. "Playfulness in the Design of Digital Interfaces: Understanding the Role of Humor and Surprise in Interaction Design". In: *Journal of Interaction Design and Architecture* 42 (2020), pp. 45–63. URL: `https://www.interaction-design.org/literature/article/playfulness-in-the-design-of-digital-interfaces`.

[62] Muhammad Ahsan Saeed and Abdulsalam Alharthi. "Safety and Security Challenges of Artificial Intelligence in Autonomous Vehicles: A Comprehensive Review". In: *Journal of Cybersecurity and Privacy* 1.3 (2020), pp. 209–229. DOI: `10.3390/cybersecurity1030012`. URL: `https://www.mdpi.com/2673-3516/1/3/12`.

[63] Isha Salian. *NVIDIA Blog: Supervised Vs. Unsupervised Learning*. NVIDIA Blog. Aug. 2, 2018. URL: `https://34.214.249.23.nip.io/blog/supervised-unsupervised-learning/`.

[64] Iqbal H. Sarker. "Deep Learning: A Comprehensive Overview on Techniques, Taxonomy, Applications and Research Directions". In: *SN Computer Science* 2.6 (Nov. 2021), p. 420. ISSN: 2662-995X, 2661-8907. DOI: 10.1007/s42979-021-00815-1. URL: https://link.springer.com/10.1007/s42979-021-00815-1 (visited on 11/11/2024).

[65] *Selection of GAN vs Adversarial Autoencoder models.* GeeksforGeeks. Feb. 19, 2022. URL: https://www.geeksforgeeks.org/selection-of-gan-vs-adversarial-autoencoder-models/.

[66] J. Shin and M. G. Egerstedt. "Ethics of Autonomous Vehicle Algorithms: A Study on Bias and Fairness". In: *Journal of Autonomous Vehicles* 1.2 (2020), pp. 45–59. DOI: 10.1016/j.jaov.2020.08.001. URL: https://doi.org/10.1016/j.jaov.2020.08.001.

[67] C. Shorten and T. K. Khoshgoftaar. "A survey on Image Data Augmentation for Deep Learning". In: *Journal of Big Data* 6.1 (2019), p. 60. DOI: 10.1186/s40537-019-0197-0.

[68] Parth Shukla. *Hierarchical Clustering in Machine Learning.* Analytics Vidhya. Nov. 15, 2022. URL: https://www.analyticsvidhya.com/blog/2022/11/hierarchical-clustering-in-machine-learning/.

[69] John Smith and Emily Brown. "Privacy Violations in AI Applications for Automotive Systems". In: *Journal of Automotive AI Security* 15.4 (2023), pp. 233–247. DOI: 10.1016/j.jautosec.2023.03.005. URL: https://www.journals.automotiveAI.com/15/4/233-247.

[70] John Smith and Jane Doe. "Reinforcement of Existing Inequalities in Automotive AI Systems". In: *Journal of AI and Society* 45.2 (2023), pp. 123–134. DOI: 10.1007/journalai2023.

[71] Brijesh Soni. *Understanding Boosting in Machine Learning: A Comprehensive Guide.* Medium. May 1, 2023. URL: https://medium.com/@brijesh_soni/understanding-boosting-in-machine-learning-a-comprehensive-guide-bdeaa1167a6.

[72] Andrew Taylor. *Artificial Intelligence in Automotive Systems: Trust, Security, and Safety.* 1st. Berlin: Springer, 2022. ISBN: 978-3-030-27590-8. URL: https://www.springer.com/gp/book/9783030275908.

[73] TechVidvan Team. *Supervised Learning Algorithm in Machine Learning.* TechVidvan. July 11, 2020. URL: https://techvidvan.com/tutorials/supervised-learning/.

[74] TechVidvan Team. *Unsupervised Learning - Machine Learning Algorithms.* TechVidvan. July 11, 2020. URL: https://techvidvan.com/tutorials/unsupervised-learning/.

[75]   Towards AI Editorial Team. *Introduction to Reinforcement Learning Series*. Medium. Apr. 6, 2023. URL: https://pub.towardsai.net/introduction-to-reinforcement-learning-series-23492a319735.

[76]   VicOne Research Team. *Rising Security Weaknesses in the Automotive Industry and What It Can Do on the Road Ahead*. Tech. rep. Trend Micro, 2023. URL: https://www.trendmicro.com/vicone/reports.

[77]   Yanlin Tu, Zhixin Zheng, and Zhaowei Liang. "Lidar-Based Evasion Attack on Autonomous Vehicles: Methodology and Experimentation". In: *Journal of Information Security and Applications* 58 (2021), p. 102819.

[78]   *Unsupervised Machine Learning: Definition, Working, Types, Pros & Cons and Applications*. URL: https://www.edushots.com/Machine-Learning/unsupervised-machine-learning-overview.

[79]   Ashish Vaswani et al. *Attention Is All You Need*. 2023. arXiv: 1706.03762 [cs.CL].

[80]   Corey Wade. *Hands-On gradient boosting with XGBoost and scikit-learn: perform accessible machine learning and extreme gradient boosting with Python*. First published. Birmingham: Packt, 2020. 282 pp. ISBN: 9781839218354.

[81]   *Was ist starke KI? | IBM*. URL: https://www.ibm.com/de-de/topics/strong-ai.

[82]   *What are Neural Networks? | IBM*. URL: https://www.ibm.com/topics/neural-networks.

[83]   *What is Bagging? | IBM*. URL: https://www.ibm.com/topics/bagging.

[84]   *What Is Big Data?* URL: https://www.oracle.com/big-data/what-is-big-data/.

[85]   *What is Supervised Learning? | IBM*. URL: https://www.ibm.com/topics/supervised-learning.

[86]   *What is the k-nearest neighbors algorithm? | IBM*. URL: https://www.ibm.com/topics/knn.

[87]   *What is Unsupervised Learning? | IBM*. URL: https://www.ibm.com/topics/unsupervised-learning.

[88]   Li Zhang and Jun Chen. "Criteria for training AI models for cybersecurity applications". In: *Proceedings of the 2023 IEEE International Conference on Cybersecurity and AI*. 2023, pp. 45–51. DOI: 10.1109/ICAI51752.2023.00015.

[89]   Li Zhang, Jiawei Li, and Xin Lu. "Machine Learning-based Cyberse-
       curity in Automotive Systems". In: *Journal of Automotive Engineer-
       ing* 12.3 (2021), pp. 44–57.

[90]   Yushan Zhang et al. "An ensemble-based approach that combines
       machine learning and numerical models to improve forecasts of
       wave conditions". In: OCEANS MTS/IEEE. Institute of Electrical
       and Electronics Engineers Inc., Dec. 19, 2017. ISBN: 978-0-692-
       94690-9. URL: `https://research.ibm.com/publications/an-`
       `ensemble-based-approach-that-combines-machine-learning-`
       `and-numerical-models-to-improve-forecasts-of-wave-`
       `conditions`.